LOW-FAT
WAYS TO COOK
DESSERTS

LOW-FAT
WAYS TO COOK
DESSERTS

COMPILED AND EDITED BY
SUSAN M. McINTOSH, M.S., R.D.

Oxmoor
House®

Library of Congress Catalog Number: 95-74600
ISBN: 0-8487-2204-3
Manufactured in the United States of America
First Printing 1995

Editor-in-Chief: Nancy Fitzpatrick Wyatt
Editorial Director, Special Interest Publications: Ann H. Harvey
Senior Foods Editor: Katherine M. Eakin
Senior Editor, Editorial Services: Olivia Kindig Wells
Art Director: James Boone

LOW-FAT WAYS TO COOK DESSERTS

Menu and Recipe Consultant: Susan McEwen McIntosh, M.S., R.D.
Assistant Editor: Kelly Hooper Troiano
Foods Editor: Anne C. Chappell, M.S., M.P.H., R.D.
Copy Editor: Shari K. Wimberly
Editorial Assistant: Julie A. Cole
Indexer: Mary Ann Laurens
Assistant Art Director: Cynthia R. Cooper
Designer: Carol Damsky
Senior Photographer: Jim Bathie
Photographers: Howard L. Puckett, *Cooking Light* magazine;
  Ralph Anderson
Senior Photo Stylist: Kay E. Clarke
Photo Stylists: Cindy Manning Barr, *Cooking Light* magazine;
  Virginia R. Cravens
Production and Distribution Director: Phillip Lee
Associate Production and Distribution Manager: John Charles Gardner
Associate Production Manager: Theresa L. Beste
Production Assistants: Valerie Heard, Marianne Jordan Wilson

Our appreciation to the staff of *Cooking Light* magazine and to the Southern
Progress Corporation library staff for their contributions to this book.

Cover: *Mocha Fudge Pie (recipe on page 96)*
Frontispiece: *Peach Trifle (recipe on page 21)*

CONTENTS

INDULGE IN DESSERT!

*Y*ou've finally decided to cut back on fat, and you've been
successful up to now—your entrée, vegetable, and even bread have
all contained less than 30 percent fat. But then comes dessert—your
favorite part of the meal. Is there a way to make healthy, low-fat
desserts that taste good?

Welcome to *Low-Fat Ways To Cook Desserts*—a collection of recipes that will satisfy your sweet tooth without sacrificing your resolutions.

In the following pages, we treat you to more than 150 desserts—from super-quick recipes such as Banana Split Smoothie (page 128) to more complicated creations like Vanilla Truffle Torte (page 71).

Once you've tried some of our favorites, you may want to lighten your own dessert recipes. Many desserts, especially baked goods like cakes and cookies, require some fat to be successful. However, with proper substitutions, you can keep the grams of fat per serving to a minimum.

SUPERMARKET SELECTIONS

To get started, stock your pantry, refrigerator, and freezer with an assortment of basic ingredients. The following information will guide you down the supermarket aisles and help you make healthy, low-fat choices.

Eggs and egg substitutes—The white of an egg contains no fat or cholesterol, but a large yolk has about 213 milligrams of cholesterol and 5 grams of fat. Today, commercial egg substitutes containing no cholesterol are available. Egg whites are the main ingredient in most egg substitutes. Sodium, oil, coloring, and preservatives are added so that the product will taste and perform like whole eggs.

Two egg whites can be used in place of a whole egg in many recipes with good results. Although some recipes work well with egg whites, others do not. So keep both egg whites and egg substitutes on hand.

Here are some tips on buying and using eggs and egg substitutes:

• Buy large eggs when buying eggs for their whites; two large whole eggs yield ¼ cup egg white.

• Examine eggs before buying to make sure they are not cracked or dirty; cracked eggs may be contaminated with salmonella bacteria and should not be used.

• Avoid buying eggs stored at room temperature.

• Remember that egg substitutes found in the freezer section should be frozen solid; if there is evidence of sweating on the carton, choose another carton.

• Be sure to cook egg substitutes slowly over low heat; they are lower in fat than whole eggs and can be tough and dry if cooked over high heat.

• Follow USDA recommendations and avoid dishes that contain raw eggs—like traditional ice cream, eggnog, and chilled soufflés made without cooking the eggs. Eggs should be cooked to an internal temperature of 160° to kill any salmonella bacteria which may be present. Egg substitute, however, has been pasteurized and is safe to use in such recipes without further cooking.

Flour—Regardless of the type, flour is essentially free of fat. All-purpose flour is the most basic ingredient for baked products and is often used to thicken sauces and puddings. Cake flour is a soft-wheat flour with a lower protein content than all-purpose flour. Products made with cake flour have a tender, delicate texture. All-purpose flour can be substituted for cake flour by using 2 tablespoons less all-purpose flour per cup.

Fruit—Fruit is naturally low in fat, high in fiber and complex carbohydrate, and a good source of vitamins and minerals. Dietitians recommend two to four servings of fruit in each day's meal plan, so load up your shopping cart with fresh fruit. Unsweetened canned fruit and frozen unsweetened fruit provide about the same nutrients as fresh but usually have less fiber than fresh, unpeeled fruit.

Choose canned or refrigerated juices that are 100 percent juice. Although fruit drinks and most fruit-flavored sodas have little or no fat, these usually have a high sugar content and are not good sources of vitamins and minerals.

Margarine—For many of our baked products, we recommend using a stick margarine as opposed to a spread or squeeze type. When selecting a regular stick margarine, choose one that lists an acceptable liquid vegetable oil such as canola, safflower, sunflower, corn, or soybean oil as the first ingredient—these have a lower ratio of saturated fat to polyunsaturated fat. (It's important to keep saturated fats low because they tend to raise blood cholesterol levels, which in turn may increase the risk of heart disease.) Make sure that the amount of saturated fat is 2 grams or less per tablespoon.

Reduced-calorie margarines and spreads usually meet the requirement for a low amount of saturated fat. Often, the first ingredient in these products is water, which has been whipped into the margarine to increase the volume without adding fat. Reduced-calorie margarine is available in tubs, squeeze bottles, and sticks.

However, substituting reduced-calorie margarine for regular butter or margarine does not work well for many baked desserts because the additional water it contains may cause sogginess.

Milk—Milk and other dairy products are the best food sources of calcium and are rich in protein, vitamins, and minerals. Most adults should have at least two servings of dairy products each day. Teenagers, young adults (to age 24), and women who are pregnant or breast feeding need at least three servings a day, and children need even more.

Whole milk and products made from it (cheese, sour cream, and ice cream) are high in fat, especially saturated fat.

Lower fat milks are described by the amount of fat they contain by weight—2 percent, 1 percent, and skim (or nonfat) milk. Two percent milk derives 35 percent of its calories from fat, which makes it too high in fat to be considered a low-fat food. One percent milk and skim milk are the best choices for heart-healthy eating. (Children under the age of two need whole milk instead of low-fat milk.)

When a recipe calls for cream or whole milk, skim milk can often be substituted. And if the recipe doesn't look creamy enough, try adding nonfat dry milk powder, a tablespoon at a time, until you reach the desired consistency.

Sour cream and yogurt—Substitute nonfat or low-fat sour cream for its higher fat counterpart. Choose nonfat or low-fat yogurt instead of that made from whole milk.

Sugars and other sweeteners—What would most desserts be without sugar or some other sweetener? Sugar contains no fat, but the calories it offers are "empty" calories, providing only simple carbohydrates but no vitamins, minerals, or fiber.

Granulated sugar is the most common form and is the kind called for when we specify "sugar" in a recipe. Other sweeteners include powdered sugar, brown sugar, molasses, honey, and corn syrup. There is no real advantage nutritionally to using one sweetener instead of another.

Vegetable oils—Selecting a vegetable oil that is free of saturated fat is impossible because all oils contain some saturated fat, though in varying amounts. The key is to find one that has a higher percentage of monounsaturated and polyunsaturated fats than saturated fats.

Canola, olive, and peanut oils are the three vegetable oils highest in monounsaturated fats. The best choices for oils high in polyunsaturated fats are safflower, sunflower, corn, and soybeans oils.

Remember that no matter what kind of vegetable oil you choose, it's going to be 100 percent fat, so choose wisely and use sparingly.

STEPS TO GREAT FINALES

Perfect cakes, cookies, and pastries are the results of accurate measuring and proper mixing and baking. To ensure your success, use the tips that follow, unless your recipe specifies something different.

CAKE-BAKING TIPS

• Position oven rack in the center of the oven, and preheat the oven.

• Use the correct pan size.

• Allow margarine and milk to reach room temperature before mixing.

• Do not sift all-purpose flour unless specified; just stir the flour lightly, spoon into a dry ingredient measuring cup, and level with the straight edge of a knife. Cake flour should always be sifted before measuring.

• Use stick margarine instead of whipped or squeeze margarine. Use reduced-calorie margarine only if the recipe specifies.

• Beat sugar into margarine until the mixture is "light and fluffy." This may take up to 7 minutes with a standard mixer and longer with a portable mixer.

• When adding dry and liquid ingredients alternately, be sure to beat after each addition, but only until the batter is smooth. Do not overbeat at this stage.

• Use a rubber spatula to scrape the sides and bottom of the bowl often during mixing.

• Arrange cakepans on the center rack so they do not touch each other or the sides of the oven. If they must be placed on separate racks, stagger the pans so air can circulate.

• Test the cake for doneness before removing it from the oven (underbaking can cause a cake to fall). To test, insert a wooden pick in the center; it should come out clean. Also, the cake should spring back when lightly touched.

• Let layer cakes cool in pans 10 minutes and tube cakes cool for 15 minutes in the pan. Then remove cakes from pans, and place on wire racks to cool completely. Allow cakes to cool completely before adding filling or frosting, unless otherwise indicated.

COOKIE-MAKING TIPS

• Cookie sheets made of heavy-weight nonrusting metal with a dull finish are best. Dark cookie sheets can cause cookies to burn on the bottom.

• Do not coat cookie sheets with cooking spray unless specified in the recipe.

• When a recipe calls for softened margarine, it should be just soft enough to blend smoothly with other ingredients.

• When rolling out dough for cut-out cookies, do not work in too much extra flour or the cookies may be tough.

• Place cut-out cookies at least 1 inch apart on the cookie sheet to allow for spreading. Drop cookies are best placed 2 inches apart.

• Allow cookies sheets to cool between batches.

• Transfer cookies to wire racks after baking to allow air to circulate and prevent the bottoms of the cookies from becoming soggy.

TIPS FOR PERFECT PASTRY

• You can cut the margarine into the flour with two knives, but a pastry blender will make the job easier. It is often helpful to chill the margarine before cutting it into the flour.

• Add the minimum amount of water that will moisten the flour mixture; too much can make pastry tough and soggy.

• Once water is added to the flour, don't overwork the dough—the more you handle it, the more gluten will develop, toughening the pastry.

• Chilling the dough makes it easier to handle and helps prevent the crust from being soggy.

• To minimize stickiness when rolling out pastry, roll the dough between two sheets of heavy-duty plastic wrap. Or roll it on a lightly floured pastry cloth, using a floured rolling pin cover on the rolling pin.

• For best results, use an ovenproof glass pieplate or a dull metal piepan. Shiny metal pans reflect heat and prevent the crust from browning.

• When baking the pastry shell without a filling, prick bottom and sides generously before baking. Do not prick shell if it is to be filled.

• Cool baked pastries on a wire rack; it will help keep crusts from becoming soggy.

FINISHING TOUCHES

Edible flowers add a crowning touch to a dessert. Check with your florist on the availability of edible flowers.

Lemon balm (top) or other varieties of mint can be colorful garnishes for many desserts.

For chocolate garnishes, make a design on wax paper. Pipe melted chocolate over design. Chill until firm.

For a quick garnish for cakes or cookies, cover with a doily. Sift powdered sugar over doily to create a lacy design.

Fresh berries and citrus rind make a colorful garnish. Select ripe, unblemished fruit to use as an accent on desserts.

For apricot roses, flatten a dried apricot, and roll into a cone. Press more apricots for petals; secure with a pick.

BAKING PAN SUBSTITUTIONS

If the recipe calls for a pan you don't have, you can often substitute one of a similar capacity.
Remember that it may be necessary to adjust the baking time.

Shape	Dimensions	Capacity	Substitutions
Rectangular	10- x 6- x 2-inch 11- x 7- x 1½-inch 13- x 9- x 2-inch	5 cups 8 cups 15 cups	8 x 1½-inch round 8- x 8- x 2-inch two 9-inch round or three 8-inch round
Square	8- x 8- x 2-inch 9- x 9- x 2-inch	8 cups 10 cups	11- x 7- x 1½-inch 9- x 5- x 3-inch loafpan or two 8-inch round
Round	8- x 1½-inch 8- x 2-inch 9- x 1½-inch	5 cups 6 cups 6 cups	10- x 6- x 2-inch 8½- x 4½- x 2½-inch loafpan 8- x 2-inch round
Tube	10- x 4-inch	16 cups	two 9- x 5- x 3-inch loafpans
Loaf	8½- x 4½- x 2½-inch 9- x 5- x 3-inch	6 cups 8 cups	two or three 6- x 3- x 2-inch loafpans three or four 6- x 3- x 2-inch loafpans
Pieplate	9- x 1½-inch 10- x 1½-inch	4 cups 6 cups	No substitution unless tart pans are used
Jellyroll Pan	15- x 10- x 1-inch	10 cups	Do not substitute baking sheet for jellyroll pan
Cookie Sheet	size varies		Baking sheet or jellyroll pan

ALCOHOL SUBSTITUTIONS

What if you do not wish to use or do not have the liqueur or wine specified in a recipe? This
chart lists substitutes for several commonly used alcoholic beverages.

If the recipe calls for:	Substitute:
2 tablespoons amaretto	¼ to ½ teaspoon almond-flavored extract*
2 tablespoons bourbon or sherry	1 to 2 teaspoons vanilla extract*
2 tablespoons brandy or rum	½ to 1 teaspoon brandy or rum extract*
2 tablespoons Grand Marnier or other orange-flavored liqueur	2 tablespoons unsweetened orange juice concentrate or 2 tablespoons orange juice and ½ teaspoon orange extract
2 tablespoons Kahlúa or other coffee- or chocolate-flavored liqueur	½ to 1 teaspoon chocolate extract plus ½ to 1 teaspoon instant coffee in 2 tablespoons water
¼ cup or more brandy, port wine, rum, sweet sherry, or fruit-flavored liqueur	Equal measure of unsweetened orange juice or apple juice plus 1 teaspoon of corresponding flavored extract or vanilla extract
¼ cup or more red wine	Equal measure of red grape juice or cranberry juice
¼ cup or more white wine	Equal measure of white grape juice or apple juice

*Water, milk, white grape juice, or apple juice may be added to get the specified amount of liquid
(for recipes in which liquid amount is crucial).

LOW-FAT BASICS

*W*hether you are trying to lose or maintain weight, low-fat eating makes good sense. Research studies show that decreasing your fat intake reduces risks of heart disease, diabetes, and some types of cancer. The goal recommended by major health groups is an intake of 30 percent or less of total daily calories.

The *Low-Fat Ways To Cook* series gives you practical, delicious recipes with realistic advice about low-fat cooking and eating. The recipes are lower in total fat than traditional recipes, and most provide less than 30 percent of calories from fat and less than 10 percent of calories from saturated fat.

Basic Pastry Shell on page 97 is an exception. Although lower in fat than a standard recipe, this pastry provides 51% of its calories as fat. However, when the pastry is combined with a low-fat filling, the recipe as a whole may be within the recommended percentage of fat. For example, Lemon Meringue Pie on page 99 calls for Basic Pastry Shell with a low-fat lemon filling. When the total pie is analyzed, fat contributes only 26% of the calories.

The goal of fat reduction need not be to eliminate all fat from your diet. In fact, a small amount of fat is needed to transport fat-soluble vitamins and maintain other normal body functions.

FIGURING THE FAT

The easiest way to achieve a diet with 30 percent or fewer of total calories from fat is to establish a daily "fat budget" based on the total number of calories you need each day. To estimate your daily calorie requirements, multiply your current weight by 15. Remember that this is only a rough guide because calorie requirements vary according to age, body size, and level of activity. To gain or lose 1 pound a week, add or subtract 500 calories a day. (A diet of fewer than 1,200 calories a day is not recommended unless medically supervised.)

Once you determine your personal daily caloric requirement, it's easy to figure the number of fat grams you should consume each day. These should equal or be lower than the number of fat grams indicated on the Daily Fat Limits chart.

DAILY FAT LIMITS		
Calories Per Day	30 Percent of Calories	Grams of Fat
1,200	360	40
1,500	450	50
1,800	540	60
2,000	600	67
2,200	660	73
2,500	750	83
2,800	840	93

NUTRITIONAL ANALYSIS

Each recipe in *Low-Fat Ways To Cook Desserts* has been kitchen-tested by a staff of qualified home economists. Registered dietitians have determined the nutrient information using a computer system that analyzes every ingredient. These efforts ensure the success of each recipe and will help you fit these recipes into your own meal planning.

The nutrient grid that follows each recipe provides calories per serving and the percentage of calories from fat. In addition, the grid lists the grams of total fat, saturated fat, protein, and carbohydrate, and the milligrams of cholesterol and sodium per serving. The nutrient values are as accurate as possible and are based on these assumptions.

• When a range is given for an ingredient (3 to 3½ cups, for instance), we calculate the lesser amount.

• When a recipe calls for "margarine," the analysis is based on regular stick margarine. If "reduced-calorie margarine" is specified, the analysis is based on reduced-calorie stick margarine, not the kind in a tub or squeeze bottle.

• Garnishes and other optional ingredients are not calculated.

• Only the amount of marinade absorbed by the food is calculated.

• Some of the alcohol calories evaporate during heating, and only those remaining are counted.

• Fruits and vegetables listed in the ingredients are not peeled unless specified.

OLD-WORLD SPECIALTIES

*F*rom the tip of Italy's boot to the northern edge of Sweden, Europe is known for its luscious desserts. We've collected a sampling of them here, each lightened of the typical cream and butter yet full of flavor.

We start our journey with buttery-tasting polenta cake from Italy and jump to France for clafouti, a cake-like fruit pudding. Across the continent are cookies as different as their countries of origin such as the two we've chosen to feature—Swedish Pepparkakor and German Lebkuchen. You'll also find Cesnica, a version of baklava that is served in Yugoslavian homes at the end of the Christmas season.

Last on the tour are three fruit desserts: an apple-topped pancake from Germany, Raspberry Coeur à la Crème from France, and Peach Trifle from England.

Torta di Polenta (recipe on page 14)

TORTA DI POLENTA

(pictured on page 12)

Polenta, a staple of northern Italy, is made from cornmeal and water. The cornmeal adds a wonderful texture to this cake.

⅔ cup sugar
3 tablespoons stick margarine, softened
2 egg yolks
2 teaspoons vanilla extract
1¾ cups yellow cornmeal
¾ cup all-purpose flour
1 teaspoon baking powder
1 teaspoon baking soda
¼ teaspoon salt
½ teaspoon ground nutmeg
1½ cups low-fat buttermilk
Vegetable cooking spray
Two-Berry Sauce

Beat sugar, margarine, and egg yolks at medium speed of an electric mixer until light and fluffy. Add vanilla; beat at low speed until well blended.

Combine cornmeal and next 5 ingredients. With mixer at low speed, add to creamed mixture alternately with buttermilk, beginning and ending with cornmeal mixture. Pour into a 9-inch round cake-pan coated with cooking spray. Bake at 350° for 40 minutes or until wooden pick inserted in center comes out clean. Cool in pan on a wire rack 10 minutes; remove from pan, and cool on rack. To serve, cut into wedges, and spoon 2 tablespoons Two-Berry Sauce over each wedge. Yield: 10 servings.

TWO-BERRY SAUCE
¾ cup frozen unsweetened blackberries, divided
¾ cup frozen unsweetened raspberries, divided
¼ cup water
¼ cup unsweetened orange juice
1 tablespoon sugar
2 teaspoons cornstarch
2 tablespoons Chambord (raspberry-flavored liqueur)

Position knife blade in food processor bowl; add half of berries, water, and orange juice. Process 1 minute or until smooth. Combine sugar and cornstarch in a small saucepan; stir well. Gradually add berry puree, stirring with a wire whisk until blended. Bring to a boil over medium heat; cook, stirring constantly, 1 minute or until thickened. Add remaining berries and Chambord; cook until thoroughly heated. Yield: 1¼ cups.

PER SERVING: 257 CALORIES (21% FROM FAT)
FAT 6.1G (SATURATED FAT 1.2G)
PROTEIN 4.8G   CARBOHYDRATE 44.9G
CHOLESTEROL 44MG   SODIUM 239MG

CHERRY CLAFOUTI

To enjoy the full flavor and just-right texture of this dish, serve it before it cools.

1 (16½-ounce) can pitted dark sweet cherries in heavy syrup, drained
Vegetable cooking spray
2⅔ cups 2% low-fat milk
¾ cup all-purpose flour
½ cup sugar
2 teaspoons vanilla extract
¼ teaspoon salt
1 egg
1 egg white
¼ cup sugar
1 tablespoon powdered sugar
2⅔ cups low-fat vanilla frozen yogurt

Place cherries in an 8-inch square baking dish or deep-dish quiche dish coated with cooking spray; set aside.

Combine milk and next 6 ingredients; stir well with a wire whisk. Pour over cherries; sprinkle with ¼ cup sugar. Bake at 375° for 1 hour and 10 minutes or until set. Dust with powdered sugar. Serve warm; top each serving with ⅓ cup frozen yogurt. Yield: 8 servings.

PER SERVING: 234 CALORIES (12% FROM FAT)
FAT 3.0G (SATURATED FAT 1.6G)
PROTEIN 6.2G   CARBOHYDRATE 46.1G
CHOLESTEROL 36MG   SODIUM 141MG

Cherry Clafouti

Swedish Pepparkakor

SWEDISH PEPPARKAKOR

⅓ cup plus 1 tablespoon stick margarine,
    softened
¾ cup sugar
1 tablespoon grated orange rind
1 tablespoon dark corn syrup
1½ teaspoons water
1 egg white
2 cups all-purpose flour
1 teaspoon baking soda
1 teaspoon ground cinnamon
½ teaspoon ground ginger
¼ teaspoon ground cloves
Vegetable cooking spray
1 cup sifted powdered sugar
1 tablespoon skim milk
½ teaspoon almond extract

Beat margarine at medium speed of an electric mixer until creamy; gradually add ¾ cup sugar, beating until light and fluffy. Add orange rind and next 3 ingredients; beat well. Combine flour and next 4 ingredients; add flour mixture to creamed mixture, beating well. Shape dough into a ball; wrap in heavy-duty plastic wrap, and freeze 30 minutes.

Divide dough in half; cover and chill half of dough. Roll remaining half of dough to ⅛-inch thickness on a lightly floured surface. Cut with a 2-inch round cookie cutter. Place on cookie sheets coated with cooking spray. Bake at 350° for 8 to 10 minutes. Cool on wire racks. Repeat procedure with remaining dough.

Combine powdered sugar, milk, and almond extract; stir well. Drizzle over cookies. Store loosely covered. Yield: 70 cookies.

PER COOKIE: 37 CALORIES (27% FROM FAT)
FAT 1.1G (SATURATED FAT 0.2G)
PROTEIN 0.4G   CARBOHYDRATE 6.7G
CHOLESTEROL 0MG   SODIUM 25MG

LEBKUCHEN

¼ cup plus 2 tablespoons stick margarine,
    softened
¼ cup sugar
¼ cup honey
1 egg, lightly beaten
2½ cups all-purpose flour
¼ teaspoon baking powder
⅛ teaspoon baking soda
⅛ teaspoon salt
1 tablespoon unsweetened cocoa
2 teaspoons ground cinnamon
1 teaspoon ground cloves
½ teaspoon ground cardamom
2 tablespoons ice water
Vegetable cooking spray
½ cup sifted powdered sugar
1½ teaspoons skim milk
½ teaspoon lemon juice

Beat margarine and ¼ cup sugar at medium speed of an electric mixer until light and fluffy (about 5 minutes). Add honey and egg; beat 2 minutes or until well blended.

Combine flour and next 7 ingredients. With mixer running at low speed, add dry ingredients to creamed mixture, beating until mixture resembles coarse meal. Sprinkle ice water, 1 tablespoon at a time, over surface; toss with a fork until dry ingredients are moistened. (Dough will be stiff.) Turn dough out onto a lightly floured surface; knead lightly 6 times. Gently press mixture into a ball; wrap in heavy-duty plastic wrap, and freeze 30 minutes.

Divide dough in half. Cover and chill half of dough. Roll remaining half to ⅛-inch thickness on a sheet of heavy-duty plastic wrap. Cut with a 3-inch star cookie cutter; place 1 inch apart on cookie sheets coated with cooking spray. Bake at 350° for 8 minutes. Cool on wire racks. Repeat procedure with remaining dough.

Combine powdered sugar, milk, and lemon juice; stir. Drizzle over cookies. Yield: 57 cookies.

PER COOKIE: 45 CALORIES (28% FROM FAT)
FAT 1.4G (SATURATED FAT 0.3G)
PROTEIN 0.7G   CARBOHYDRATE 7.5G
CHOLESTEROL 4MG   SODIUM 23MG

Cesnica

CESNICA

Butter-flavored vegetable cooking spray
6 sheets frozen phyllo pastry, thawed
¾ cup golden raisins
¼ cup plus 2 tablespoons chopped walnuts,
   toasted
2 tablespoons stick margarine, melted
½ cup honey
¼ cup water
1 teaspoon fresh lemon juice

Coat an 8-inch round cakepan with cooking spray; set aside.

Stack phyllo sheets; cut in half crosswise. Gently press 1 half-sheet of phyllo into cakepan, allowing ends to extend over edges of pan; lightly coat phyllo with cooking spray. Place another half-sheet of phyllo across first sheet to form a crisscross design; lightly coat phyllo with cooking spray. Repeat procedure with another half-sheet of phyllo and cooking spray.

Sprinkle 2 tablespoons raisins and 1 tablespoon walnuts over phyllo. Place another half-sheet of phyllo in pan, continuing crisscross design; lightly coat phyllo with cooking spray. Sprinkle 2 tablespoons raisins and 1 tablespoon walnuts over phyllo. Repeat procedure with 5 half-sheets of phyllo, cooking spray, remaining ½ cup raisins, and remaining ¼ cup walnuts, ending with phyllo coated with cooking spray.

Lightly coat 1 side of remaining 3 half-sheets of phyllo, and gently layer each into cakepan to form a crisscross design, allowing ends to extend over edges of pan. Fold in edges of phyllo to fit pan and form a rim.

Score diamond shapes into top layers of phyllo, using a sharp knife. Drizzle margarine over phyllo. Bake at 350° for 25 minutes or until golden.

Combine honey, water, and lemon juice in a saucepan; bring to a boil. Reduce heat; simmer, uncovered, 10 minutes, stirring frequently. Remove from heat; drizzle honey mixture over phyllo. Cool completely in pan. Yield: 10 servings.

PER SERVING: 172 CALORIES (30% FROM FAT)
FAT 5.7G (SATURATED FAT 0.7G)
PROTEIN 2.4G   CARBOHYDRATE 30.4G
CHOLESTEROL 0MG   SODIUM 84MG

DESSERT PANCAKE WITH APPLE TOPPING

1 cup all-purpose flour
2 cups 1% low-fat milk, divided
2 tablespoons sugar
1 teaspoon vanilla extract
¼ teaspoon almond extract
3 eggs, lightly beaten
Dash of salt
Vegetable cooking spray
1 teaspoon margarine
1 tablespoon powdered sugar
Apple Topping

Combine flour and 1 cup milk in a large bowl; stir well with a wire whisk. Add remaining 1 cup milk and next 5 ingredients. Stir well; set aside.

Coat a 9-inch pieplate with cooking spray; add margarine. Bake at 450° for 1 minute. Remove pieplate from oven, and tilt in all directions to coat bottom. Pour egg mixture into pieplate; bake 5 minutes. Reduce heat to 425°; bake an additional 20 minutes or until puffed and golden. Remove from oven; sprinkle with powdered sugar. Spoon Apple Topping into the center; serve immediately. Yield: 8 servings.

APPLE TOPPING
2 teaspoons margarine
3 medium Granny Smith apples, peeled and
   thinly sliced
2 tablespoons sugar
½ teaspoon grated lemon rind
1 tablespoon fresh lemon juice
½ teaspoon ground cinnamon
¼ teaspoon ground nutmeg

Melt margarine in a large skillet over medium-high heat. Add remaining ingredients; cook 7 minutes or until tender, stirring occasionally. Yield: 8 (¼-cup) servings.

PER SERVING: 183 CALORIES (22% FROM FAT)
FAT 4.4G (SATURATED FAT 1.4G)
PROTEIN 6.1G   CARBOHYDRATE 29.8G
CHOLESTEROL 85MG   SODIUM 91MG

Raspberry Coeur à la Crème

RASPBERRY COEUR À LA CRÈME

Low-fat yogurt and Neufchâtel cheese keep the fat low in this classic French "heart with cream."

1 (10-ounce) package frozen raspberries in light syrup, thawed
1 cup skim milk
1 envelope unflavored gelatin
½ (8-ounce) package Neufchâtel cheese, softened
¼ cup sugar
1 (8-ounce) carton raspberry low-fat yogurt
Vegetable cooking spray
2 teaspoons cornstarch
Fresh raspberries (optional)

Drain raspberries, reserving syrup. Set aside.

Combine milk and 2 tablespoons reserved raspberry syrup in a small saucepan. Sprinkle gelatin over milk mixture; let stand 1 minute. Cook over low heat, stirring constantly, until gelatin dissolves. Remove from heat, and let cool.

Position knife blade in food processor bowl. Add cheese, sugar, yogurt, and gelatin mixture; process until smooth. Pour mixture into a 4-cup heart-shaped mold coated with cooking spray. Cover and chill until firm.

Combine remaining raspberry syrup and cornstarch in a small nonaluminum saucepan; stir with a wire whisk until well blended. Bring to a boil; cook over medium heat, stirring constantly, until thickened. Gently stir in reserved raspberries; cover and chill. Unmold gelatin mixture onto a large serving platter. Garnish with fresh raspberries, if desired. Serve with raspberry sauce. Yield: 6 servings.

PER SERVING: 190 CALORIES (24% FROM FAT)
FAT 5.1G (SATURATED FAT 3.1G)
PROTEIN 6.1G   CARBOHYDRATE 31.1G
CHOLESTEROL 17MG   SODIUM 119MG

PEACH TRIFLE

(pictured on page 2)

1 (8-ounce) carton vanilla low-fat yogurt
1 (3.4-ounce) package vanilla instant pudding mix
2 cups skim milk
⅓ cup strawberry jam
1 tablespoon dry sherry
8 ounces angel food cake, cut into ¾-inch cubes and divided
2 cups canned sliced peaches in juice, drained and divided
Fresh sliced strawberries (optional)
Fresh mint sprigs (optional)

Spoon yogurt onto several layers of heavy-duty paper towels; spread to ½-inch thickness. Cover with additional paper towels; let stand 5 minutes. Scrape yogurt into a bowl, using a rubber spatula.

Combine pudding mix and skim milk; stir until blended. Stir yogurt into pudding mixture; set aside.

Combine jam and sherry, stirring with a wire whisk until blended; set aside.

Arrange half of cake cubes in a 2-quart trifle bowl. Spread half of pudding mixture over cake. Drizzle jam mixture evenly over pudding. Arrange 1 cup of sliced peaches over jam mixture. Repeat layering procedure with remaining cake, pudding, and peaches. If desired, garnish with sliced strawberries and mint sprigs. Yield: 8 servings.

PER SERVING: 226 CALORIES (2% FROM FAT)
FAT 0.6G (SATURATED FAT 0.3G)
PROTEIN 5.5G   CARBOHYDRATE 50.6G
CHOLESTEROL 3MG   SODIUM 185MG

Did You Know?

The traditional trifle from England contains ladyfingers soaked with sherry, covered with jam and custard, and topped with whipped cream and fruit. Our version is just as elegant but has been stripped of most of the fat.

ALL-OCCASION CAKES

*W*hat's a birthday without cake? Just because you're on the low-fat bandwagon, you need not deprive yourself. These cake recipes are lightened of excess fat, yet yummy enough for an 8-year-old's birthday party.

You'll find basic layers to top with a simple frosting or to dress up as an elegant torte. Next are easy-to-make cupcakes, sheet cakes, Bundt, and pound cakes. Sponge and angel food cakes, which are naturally low in fat, start on page 39. Before you start any of these cakes, however, you may want to review the recommended baking techniques on page 8.

Any lover of cheesecake is aware of its high-fat reputation. But reduced-fat versions of cream cheese and sour cream have made low-fat cheesecake a delicious reality. Be sure to try all three varieties on pages 42 and 43.

Chocolate Torte (recipe on page 25)

BASIC WHITE CAKE LAYERS

To make superfine sugar, place granulated sugar in a blender; process until finely ground.

Vegetable cooking spray
2 teaspoons cake flour
1¾ cups sifted cake flour
2 teaspoons baking powder
1 cup superfine sugar
½ cup skim milk
⅓ cup vegetable oil
1 teaspoon vanilla extract
6 egg whites
1 teaspoon cream of tartar

Coat 2 (9-inch) round cakepans or 2 (8-inch) square cakepans with cooking spray; line bottom of each pan with wax paper. Coat wax paper with cooking spray, and dust with 2 teaspoons flour. Set pans aside.

Combine 1¾ cups flour, baking powder, and sugar in a large bowl, stirring well. Combine milk, oil, and vanilla in a small bowl, stirring well. Add milk mixture to flour mixture, stirring well.

Beat egg whites at high speed of an electric mixer just until egg whites are foamy. Add cream of tartar, and beat until stiff peaks form. Gently fold one-third of beaten egg whites into batter; gently fold in remaining beaten egg whites.

Pour batter evenly into prepared pans. Bake at 350° for 20 to 22 minutes or until a wooden pick inserted in center comes out clean. Cool in pans on wire racks 10 minutes; remove from pans, and peel off wax paper. Cool layers completely on wire racks. Yield: 12 servings.

PER SERVING: 191 CALORIES (29% FROM FAT)
FAT 6.2G (SATURATED FAT 1.1G)
PROTEIN 3.4G   CARBOHYDRATE 30.3G
CHOLESTEROL 0MG   SODIUM 99MG

CHOCOLATE CAKE LAYERS

Frost these layers with Fluffy Frosting or Creamy Chocolate Frosting on page 25.

½ cup stick margarine, softened
1½ cups sugar
2 egg whites
1 egg
1 cup nonfat buttermilk
½ cup water
2 cups all-purpose flour
1 teaspoon baking soda
¼ teaspoon salt
¼ cup unsweetened cocoa
Vegetable cooking spray

Beat margarine at medium speed of an electric mixer until creamy; add sugar, beating until fluffy. Add egg whites and egg, one at a time, beating after each addition.

Combine buttermilk and water. Combine flour and next 3 ingredients; add to margarine mixture alternately with buttermilk mixture. Mix after each addition.

Pour batter into 2 (8-inch) round cakepans coated with cooking spray. Bake at 350° for 22 minutes or until a wooden pick inserted in center comes out clean. Cool in pans on wire racks 10 minutes; remove from pans. Let cool. Yield: 12 servings.

PER SERVING: 267 CALORIES (29% FROM FAT)
FAT 8.6G (SATURATED FAT 1.9G)
PROTEIN 4.7G   CARBOHYDRATE 43.3G
CHOLESTEROL 19MG   SODIUM 280MG

FLUFFY FROSTING

This frosting is called for in the Lemon-Filled Sponge Cake recipe on page 39.

1 cup sugar
¼ cup plus 2 tablespoons water
¼ teaspoon cream of tartar
Dash of salt
2 egg whites
1 teaspoon vanilla extract

Combine all ingredients except vanilla in top of a large double boiler. Beat at low speed of an electric mixer 30 seconds or just until blended.

Place over boiling water. Beat mixture constantly at high speed of an electric mixer 7 to 9 minutes or until stiff peaks form and temperature reaches 160°. Remove from heat. Add vanilla; beat 1 minute or until frosting is of spreading consistency. Yield: 4½ cups.

PER TABLESPOON: 11 CALORIES (0% FROM FAT)
FAT 0.0G (SATURATED FAT 0.0G)
PROTEIN 0.1G   CARBOHYDRATE 2.8G
CHOLESTEROL 0MG   SODIUM 3MG

CREAMY CHOCOLATE FROSTING

3 cups sifted powdered sugar
¼ cup unsweetened cocoa
¼ teaspoon salt
¼ cup skim milk
1½ teaspoons vanilla extract

Combine all ingredients; stir until frosting is of spreading consistency. Spread over cake layers, cupcakes, or brownies. Yield: 1¼ cups.

PER TABLESPOON: 77 CALORIES (2% FROM FAT)
FAT 0.2G (SATURATED FAT 0.1G)
PROTEIN 0.4G   CARBOHYDRATE 18.7G
CHOLESTEROL 0MG   SODIUM 32MG

CHOCOLATE TORTE

(pictured on page 22)

For another chocolate-raspberry combination, see the layer cake recipe on page 27—it starts with a cake mix.

Chocolate Cake Layers (see page 24)
¾ cup no-sugar-added raspberry spread
⅔ cup unsweetened cocoa
½ cup sugar
¼ cup cornstarch
1 cup 1% low-fat milk
¼ teaspoon vanilla extract
Fresh raspberries (optional)
Fresh mint sprigs (optional)

Prepare Chocolate Cake Layers; let cool.
Stir raspberry spread well. Slice each cake layer in half horizontally. Place 1 layer on plate; spread with ¼ cup raspberry spread. Repeat with next 2 layers; top with fourth layer. Cover and chill.

Combine cocoa, sugar, and cornstarch in top of a double boiler. Stir in milk. Bring water to a boil. Reduce heat to low; cook, stirring constantly, 18 minutes or until frosting is of spreading consistency. Stir in vanilla. Cover and chill. Spread frosting on top and sides of cake. If desired, garnish with raspberries and mint. Yield: 12 servings.

PER SERVING: 349 CALORIES (24% FROM FAT)
FAT 9.5G (SATURATED FAT 2.4G)
PROTEIN 6.7G   CARBOHYDRATE 60.0G
CHOLESTEROL 20MG   SODIUM 296MG

FYI

Most cake batters can be baked as cupcakes. Fill paper-lined muffin cups two-thirds full, and bake at 350° for 15 to 20 minutes or until a wooden pick inserted in center comes out clean. Remove cupcakes from pans immediately, and cool on wire racks. Most 2-layer cake recipes yield 24 to 30 cupcakes.

Raspberry-Filled Layer Cake

Raspberry-Filled Layer Cake

1 (18.25-ounce) package light white cake mix
Vegetable cooking spray
4 (1-ounce) squares semisweet chocolate, divided
2½ cups unsweetened frozen raspberries, thawed
¼ cup sugar
¾ cup plus 1 tablespoon water, divided
2 tablespoons cornstarch
¼ cup no-sugar-added seedless raspberry spread
3 tablespoons light-colored corn syrup
2 tablespoons margarine
Chocolate curls (optional)

Prepare cake mix according to package directions, reserving 2½ cups batter in a bowl. Pour remaining batter into a 9-inch round cakepan coated with cooking spray.

Melt 1 chocolate square; stir into reserved 2½ cups batter. Pour chocolate batter into a second 9-inch round cakepan coated with cooking spray. Bake cake at 350° for 25 minutes or until a wooden pick inserted in center of each comes out clean. Cool in pans on wire racks 10 minutes; remove from pans. Cool completely on wire racks.

Combine raspberries, sugar, and ½ cup water in a medium saucepan; cook over medium heat 5 minutes, stirring occasionally.

Combine ¼ cup water and cornstarch, stirring well; add to raspberry mixture. Bring to a boil, and cook 1 minute, stirring constantly with a wire whisk. Remove from heat; stir in raspberry spread. Let cool to room temperature.

Split each cake layer in half horizontally, using a serrated knife; place 1 chocolate layer, cut side up, on a serving plate. Spread with ⅔ cup raspberry mixture; top with 1 white cake layer. Repeat procedure with remaining cake layers and raspberry mixture, ending with a white cake layer.

Combine remaining 3 chocolate squares, 1 tablespoon water, corn syrup, and margarine in the top of a double boiler. Cook mixture over simmering water until chocolate melts, stirring occasionally.

Chill 15 minutes or until chocolate is spreadable. Spread glaze over top and sides of cake. Garnish with chocolate curls, if desired. Yield: 16 servings.

Per Serving: 217 Calories (22% from Fat)
Fat 5.4g (Saturated Fat 2.1g)
Protein 2.8g   Carbohydrate 41.2g
Cholesterol 0mg   Sodium 332mg

Double-Chocolate Cupcakes

1 (18.25-ounce) package light, 94%-fat-free devil's food cake mix
1 cup water
3 eggs
Vegetable cooking spray
¼ cup semisweet chocolate morsels
¼ cup skim milk
3 tablespoons unsweetened cocoa
2 cups sifted powdered sugar
2 teaspoons vanilla extract
2 tablespoons powdered sugar

Combine cake mix, water, and eggs in a bowl; beat at medium speed of an electric mixer 2 minutes. Divide batter among 24 muffins pans coated with cooking spray. Bake at 350° for 20 minutes or until a wooden pick inserted in center comes out clean. Cool in pans on wire racks 10 minutes; remove from pans, and let cool on wire racks.

Split each cupcake in half horizontally, using a serrated knife; set aside.

Combine chocolate morsels, milk, and cocoa in the top of a double boiler; bring water to a boil. Reduce heat to low; cook until chocolate morsels melt, stirring occasionally. Remove from heat; stir in 2 cups powdered sugar and vanilla. Spread bottom half of each cupcake with 2 teaspoons chocolate mixture; place top half of cupcake on chocolate mixture. Sift 2 tablespoons powdered sugar over tops of cupcakes. Yield: 2 dozen.

Per Cupcake: 155 Calories (17% from Fat)
Fat 2.9g (Saturated Fat 1.1g)
Protein 2.1g   Carbohydrate 30.2g
Cholesterol 27mg   Sodium 175mg

Applesauce Spice Cupcakes

APPLESAUCE SPICE CUPCAKES

3 cups sifted cake flour
2½ teaspoons baking powder
1 teaspoon baking soda
½ teaspoon salt
½ teaspoon ground ginger
1½ cups sugar
½ cup frozen egg substitute, thawed
½ cup skim milk
⅓ cup vegetable oil
1½ cups cinnamon applesauce
2 teaspoons vanilla extract
3 egg whites
2 teaspoons powdered sugar
⅛ teaspoon ground cinnamon

Combine first 6 ingredients in a large bowl; make a well in center of mixture.

Combine egg substitute, milk, and oil; add to dry ingredients, stirring just until moistened. Stir in applesauce and vanilla.

Beat egg whites at high speed of an electric mixer until stiff peaks form. Gently fold beaten egg white into applesauce mixture.

Spoon batter into paper-lined muffin pans, filling each three-fourths full. Bake at 400° for 16 to 18 minutes or until a wooden pick inserted in center comes out clean. Remove from pans immediately, and let cool completely on wire racks. Combine powdered sugar and cinnamon; sift evenly over cupcakes. Yield: 2 dozen.

PER CUPCAKE: 145 CALORIES (19% FROM FAT)
FAT 3.1G (SATURATED FAT 0.6G)
PROTEIN 2.2G   CARBOHYDRATE 27.2G
CHOLESTEROL 0MG   SODIUM 119MG

BANANA CAKE

For a special effect, sift powdered sugar through a paper doily onto the cooled cake.

Vegetable cooking spray
2½ cups plus 1 tablespoon sifted cake flour, divided
1½ teaspoons baking powder
½ teaspoon baking soda
1½ cups mashed ripe banana (about 4 medium)
¾ cup sugar
⅓ cup nonfat buttermilk
¼ cup vegetable oil
1 egg yolk
2 teaspoons vanilla extract
3 egg whites
¼ teaspoon cream of tartar
1 tablespoon powdered sugar

Coat a 13- x 9- x 2-inch baking dish with cooking spray; dust with 1 tablespoon cake flour, and set aside. Combine remaining 2½ cups flour, baking powder, and soda in a large mixing bowl, stirring well. Set aside.

Position knife blade in food processor bowl; add banana and next 5 ingredients. Process until smooth. Add banana mixture to flour mixture; stir gently until almost smooth. Set aside.

Beat egg whites and cream of tartar at high speed of an electric mixer just until stiff peaks form. Fold one-third of beaten egg white into batter. Gently fold in remaining egg white.

Spoon batter into prepared pan. Bake at 350° for 30 minutes or until cake springs back when lightly touched. Remove from oven, and let cool completely on a wire rack. Sift powdered sugar over cooled cake. Yield: 12 servings.

PER SERVING: 217 CALORIES (22% FROM FAT)
FAT 5.4G (SATURATED FAT 1.1G)
PROTEIN 3.5G   CARBOHYDRATE 39.0G
CHOLESTEROL 18MG   SODIUM 98MG

CARROT CAKE

1 (8-ounce) can crushed pineapple, undrained
2½ cups sifted cake flour
2 teaspoons baking soda
⅛ teaspoon salt
1 teaspoon ground cinnamon
½ teaspoon ground allspice
¼ teaspoon ground nutmeg
¾ cup firmly packed brown sugar
3 tablespoons vegetable oil
4 egg whites
⅔ cup skim milk
3 cups shredded carrot
2½ teaspoons vanilla extract, divided
Vegetable cooking spray
1 egg white
¼ teaspoon cream of tartar
½ cup sugar
1 (8-ounce) package Neufchâtel cheese
½ (8-ounce) package nonfat cream cheese

Drain pineapple, reserving 2 tablespoons juice; set aside.

Combine flour and next 5 ingredients. Combine brown sugar, oil, and 4 egg whites; beat well. Add flour mixture to brown sugar mixture alternately with milk. Mix after each addition. Stir in pineapple, carrot, and 2 teaspoons vanilla. Pour into a 13- x 9- x 2-inch pan coated with cooking spray. Bake at 350° for 30 minutes. Let cool in pan.

Beat 1 egg white and cream of tartar at high speed of an electric mixer until soft peaks form. Combine ½ cup sugar and reserved juice in a saucepan. Bring to a boil, stirring constantly; cook, without stirring, over medium heat 3 minutes or until candy thermometer registers 238°. Pour mixture in a thin stream over egg white, beating constantly at high speed. Beat at high speed 7 minutes.

Combine cheeses and remaining ½ teaspoon vanilla; beat at high speed until fluffy. Add one-third of egg white mixture; beat just until blended. Fold in remaining egg white mixture. Spread over cake. Yield: 16 servings.

PER SERVING: 223 CALORIES (25% FROM FAT)
FAT 6.1G (SATURATED FAT 2.6G)
PROTEIN 6.5G   CARBOHYDRATE 35.3G
CHOLESTEROL 13MG   SODIUM 299MG

CRANBERRY COFFEE CAKE

½ cup reduced-calorie stick margarine, softened
⅔ cup sugar
1 egg
1 teaspoon vanilla extract
1¼ cups all-purpose flour
2 teaspoons baking powder
¼ cup skim milk
2 egg whites
Vegetable cooking spray
1 cup jellied whole berry cranberry sauce
3 tablespoons sugar
2 tablespoons regular oats, uncooked
1 tablespoon brown sugar
¾ teaspoon ground allspice

Beat margarine at medium speed of an electric mixer until creamy; gradually add ⅔ cup sugar, beating well. Add 1 egg and vanilla; beat well.

Combine flour and baking powder; add to margarine mixture alternately with milk, beginning and ending with flour mixture. Mix after each addition.

Beat egg whites at high speed of an electric mixer until stiff peaks form. Gently fold egg whites into batter. Spoon half of batter into an 8-inch square pan coated with cooking spray.

Combine cranberry sauce and 3 tablespoons sugar; spoon over batter. Spoon remaining batter over cranberry mixture.

Combine oats, brown sugar, and allspice. Sprinkle oat mixture evenly over batter. Bake at 350° for 45 to 50 minutes or until a wooden pick inserted in center comes out clean. Let cool in pan on a wire rack 10 minutes. Serve warm. Yield: 9 servings.

PER SERVING: 264 CALORIES (26% FROM FAT)
FAT 7.5G (SATURATED FAT 0.2G)
PROTEIN 3.8G   CARBOHYDRATE 47.3G
CHOLESTEROL 25MG   SODIUM 130MG

Cranberry Coffee Cake

OLD-FASHIONED GINGERBREAD

⅓ cup stick margarine, softened
½ cup sugar
1 cup molasses
1 egg
2½ cups all-purpose flour
1½ teaspoons baking soda
½ teaspoon salt
1 teaspoon ground ginger
1 teaspoon ground cinnamon
½ teaspoon ground cloves
1 cup hot water
Vegetable cooking spray
Warm Lemon Glaze

Beat margarine at medium speed of an electric mixer until creamy; gradually add sugar, beating well. Add molasses and egg; beat well.

Combine flour and next 5 ingredients; add flour mixture to creamed mixture alternately with water, beginning and ending with flour mixture. Mix after each addition.

Pour batter into a 9-inch square pan coated with cooking spray. Bake at 350° for 40 minutes or until a wooden pick inserted in center comes out clean. Cool in pan 10 minutes; pour Warm Lemon Glaze over cake. Cut into squares; serve immediately. Yield: 12 servings.

WARM LEMON GLAZE
1 cup sifted powdered sugar
¼ teaspoon grated lemon rind
1½ tablespoons fresh lemon juice
1½ teaspoons water
½ teaspoon vanilla extract

Combine all ingredients in a saucepan; cook over low heat, stirring frequently, until sugar is melted and mixture is warm. Yield: ⅓ cup.

PER SERVING: 289 CALORIES (18% FROM FAT)
FAT 5.8G (SATURATED FAT 1.2G)
PROTEIN 3.3G   CARBOHYDRATE 56.6G
CHOLESTEROL 18MG   SODIUM 270MG

CHRISTMAS FRUITCAKE

¾ cup maraschino cherries, undrained
1 (16-ounce) jar ready-to-serve prunes in heavy syrup, undrained
1¼ cups sugar
¾ cup shortening
4 eggs
1 cup chopped walnuts
3 tablespoons whiskey
1 (15¼-ounce) can unsweetened crushed pineapple, undrained
1 (15-ounce) package raisins (about 2½ cups)
4 cups all-purpose flour
2 teaspoons baking soda
½ teaspoon salt
1 tablespoon ground cinnamon
1 teaspoon ground cloves
Vegetable cooking spray

Drain cherries, reserving 3 tablespoons juice. Cut cherries in half. Drain prunes, reserving ¼ cup plus 2 tablespoons syrup; pit prunes, and set aside.

Beat sugar, shortening, and eggs at medium speed of an electric mixer 2 minutes or until smooth. Stir in cherries, reserved cherry juice, prunes, reserved prune syrup, walnuts, and next 3 ingredients. Combine flour and next 4 ingredients; add to sugar mixture, and stir well.

Spoon batter into a 10-inch tube pan coated with cooking spray. Bake at 350° for 1 hour and 15 minutes or until a wooden pick inserted in center comes out clean. Let cool in pan 10 minutes on a wire rack; remove from pan, and let cool completely on a wire rack. Store tightly wrapped in heavy-duty plastic wrap. Yield: 24 servings.

Note: One (8-ounce) package bite-sized prunes can be substituted for the ready-to-serve prunes. To stew prunes, combine prunes and 2 cups water in a medium saucepan, and bring to a boil. Cover, reduce heat, and simmer 10 minutes or until tender. Drain, reserving ¼ cup plus 2 tablespoons cooking liquid to use in place of the drained syrup.

PER SERVING: 299 CALORIES (29% FROM FAT)
FAT 9.5G (SATURATED FAT 1.9G)
PROTEIN 4.9G   CARBOHYDRATE 50.8G
CHOLESTEROL 37MG   SODIUM 168MG

Christmas Fruitcake

Lemon-Poppy Seed Cake

LEMON-POPPY SEED CAKE

Be careful not to pack the flour when spooning it into the measuring cup.

1¼ cups sugar
⅓ cup vegetable oil
2 eggs
1¼ cups skim milk
¼ cup fresh lemon juice
3 cups all-purpose flour
1 teaspoon baking powder
1 teaspoon baking soda
¼ teaspoon salt
2½ tablespoons poppy seeds
1 tablespoon grated lemon rind
2 teaspoons vanilla extract
Vegetable cooking spray
⅓ cup sifted powdered sugar
1 teaspoon grated lemon rind
2 teaspoons fresh lemon juice
½ teaspoon skim milk

Combine 1¼ cups sugar and oil in a large bowl, beating well at medium speed of an electric mixer. Add eggs, one at a time, beating well after each addition.

Combine 1¼ cups milk and ¼ cup lemon juice; set aside.

Combine flour and next 4 ingredients; add to sugar mixture alternately with milk mixture, beginning and ending with flour mixture. Mix after each addition. Stir in 1 tablespoon lemon rind and vanilla.

Pour batter into a 12-cup Bundt pan coated with cooking spray. Bake at 350° for 45 minutes or until a wooden pick inserted in center comes out clean. Cool in pan on a wire rack 10 minutes; remove from pan. Let cool completely on a wire rack.

Combine powdered sugar and remaining ingredients; stir well. Brush glaze over cake. Yield: 16 servings.

PER SERVING: 223 CALORIES (25% FROM FAT)
FAT 6.1G (SATURATED FAT 1.2G)
PROTEIN 4.2G   CARBOHYDRATE 37.9G
CHOLESTEROL 28MG   SODIUM 135MG

BUTTER PECAN BUNDT CAKE

⅓ cup stick margarine
½ cup chopped pecans
3 cups plus 1 tablespoon all-purpose flour, divided
1 cup light-colored corn syrup
½ cup firmly packed brown sugar
1 egg
2 egg whites
¾ teaspoon baking soda
¼ teaspoon salt
1 cup nonfat buttermilk
1 teaspoon vanilla extract
Vegetable cooking spray
¼ cup sifted powdered sugar
1 tablespoon brown sugar
2 teaspoons skim milk

Melt margarine in a small saucepan over medium heat; add pecans, and sauté 4 minutes or until browned. Drain pecans, reserving margarine; set margarine aside. Combine pecans and 1 tablespoon flour; stir well, and set aside.

Combine reserved margarine, corn syrup, and ½ cup brown sugar in a large bowl, beating well at medium speed of an electric mixer. Add egg; beat well. Add egg whites, and beat well.

Combine remaining 3 cups flour, soda, and salt; add to brown sugar mixture alternately with buttermilk, beginning and ending with flour mixture. Mix well after each addition. Stir in pecans and vanilla.

Pour batter into a 12-cup Bundt pan coated with cooking spray. Bake at 350° for 45 minutes or until a wooden pick inserted in center comes out clean. Cool in pan on wire rack 10 minutes; remove from pan. Let cool completely on a wire rack.

Combine powdered sugar, 1 tablespoon brown sugar, and skim milk; stir well. Drizzle over cake. Yield: 16 servings.

PER SERVING: 255 CALORIES (24% FROM FAT)
FAT 6.9G (SATURATED FAT 1.1G)
PROTEIN 4.2G   CARBOHYDRATE 44.0G
CHOLESTEROL 14MG   SODIUM 196MG

CHOCOLATE-ALMOND MARBLED POUND CAKE

¼ cup stick margarine, softened
3 tablespoons shortening
1⅓ cups sugar
3 egg whites
1 cup nonfat buttermilk
½ teaspoon baking soda
2¼ cups sifted cake flour
⅛ teaspoon salt
¾ teaspoon almond extract
1 (1-ounce) square semisweet chocolate, melted
Baking spray with flour

Beat margarine and shortening at medium speed of an electric mixer until creamy; gradually add sugar, beating at high speed until light and fluffy (about 5 minutes). Add egg whites, one at a time, beating after each addition.

Combine buttermilk and soda, and set aside. Combine flour and salt; with mixer at low speed, add flour mixture to creamed mixture alternately with buttermilk mixture, beginning and ending with flour mixture. Reserve 2 cups batter; pour remaining batter into a bowl.

Stir almond extract into reserved 2 cups batter; stir chocolate into remaining batter. Spoon almond batter alternately with chocolate batter into a 9- x 5- x 3-inch loafpan coated with baking spray. Using the tip of a knife, swirl batters together. Bake at 325° for 1 hour and 10 minutes or until a wooden pick inserted in center comes out clean. Cool in pan 10 minutes on a wire rack; remove from pan, and let cool completely on a wire rack. Yield: 16 servings.

PER SERVING: 180 CALORIES (28% FROM FAT)
FAT 5.6G (SATURATED FAT 1.5G)
PROTEIN 2.6G   CARBOHYDRATE 30.4G
CHOLESTEROL 1MG   SODIUM 104MG

BLACK FOREST TRIFLE

¼ cup plus 2 tablespoons sugar
¼ cup unsweetened cocoa
3½ tablespoons cornstarch
2 cups 1% low-fat milk
1 tablespoon margarine
¾ teaspoon vanilla extract
1 (15-ounce) loaf fat-free chocolate pound cake
¼ cup Kirsch or other cherry-flavored liqueur
1 (20-ounce) can light cherry pie filling
2 cups frozen reduced-calorie whipped topping, thawed
Fresh cherries (optional)
Chocolate curls (optional)

Combine first 3 ingredients in a saucepan. Gradually add milk, stirring with a wire whisk until smooth. Cook over medium heat, stirring constantly, 5 to 8 minutes until mixture is thickened. Remove from heat. Add margarine and vanilla, stirring until margarine melts. Cover and chill.

Cut cake into 1-inch cubes. Arrange half of cake cubes in a 3-quart trifle bowl; brush with 2 tablespoons liqueur. Spoon half of cherry filling over cake. Spread half of chocolate mixture over cherry filling. Top with half of whipped topping. Repeat layers with remaining cake cubes, liqueur, cherry filling, chocolate mixture, and whipped topping. Cover and chill at least 8 hours. If desired, garnish with fresh cherries and chocolate curls. Yield: 12 servings.

PER SERVING: 234 CALORIES (12% FROM FAT)
FAT 3.0G (SATURATED FAT 1.6G)
PROTEIN 3.9G   CARBOHYDRATE 41.3G
CHOLESTEROL 2MG   SODIUM 220MG

Black Forest Trifle

Lemon-Filled Sponge Cake with Fluffy Frosting

LEMON-FILLED SPONGE CAKE WITH FLUFFY FROSTING

Basic Sponge Cake
Lemon Filling
Fluffy Frosting (see page 25)
Lemon slices and rind strips (optional)

Bake Basic Sponge Cake batter as directed. Invert pan; cool completely. Loosen cake from sides of pan, using a narrow metal spatula. Remove sides of pan, leaving cake on tube.

Using a serrated knife, split cake into thirds horizontally; remove layers from tube. Place bottom layer, cut side up, on a serving plate. Spread with 1 cup Lemon Filling; top with middle cake layer. Spread with remaining Lemon Filling; top with remaining cake layer. Spread Fluffy Frosting over top and sides. If desired, garnish with lemon slices and rind strips. Store loosely covered in refrigerator. Yield: 12 servings.

LEMON FILLING
¼ cup plus 2 tablespoons sugar
3 tablespoons cornstarch
⅛ teaspoon salt
1⅓ cups 2% low-fat milk
2 tablespoons margarine
1 teaspoon grated lemon rind
¼ cup plus 2 tablespoons fresh lemon juice

Combine sugar, cornstarch, and salt in a saucepan. Gradually add milk, stirring with a wire whisk until well blended. Add margarine. Bring to a boil over medium heat, and cook 1 minute or until thickened, stirring constantly. Remove from heat; stir in lemon rind and lemon juice. Pour into a bowl; cover and chill. Yield: 2 cups.

PER SERVING: 254 CALORIES (13% FROM FAT)
FAT 3.8G (SATURATED FAT 1.1G)
PROTEIN 4.4G   CARBOHYDRATE 51.0G
CHOLESTEROL 57MG   SODIUM 156MG

BASIC SPONGE CAKE

1 cup sifted cake flour
1 teaspoon baking powder
¼ teaspoon salt
3 eggs, separated
1 cup sugar, divided
2 teaspoons vanilla extract
¼ cup water
2 egg whites

Combine cake flour, baking powder, and salt; stir well, and set aside. Beat 3 egg yolks in a large mixing bowl at high speed of an electric mixer for 1 minute. Add ¾ cup sugar, beating constantly until egg yolks are thick and pale (about 5 minutes). Add vanilla and water; beat at low speed until blended. Add flour mixture to egg yolk mixture, beating at low speed until blended; set aside.

Beat 5 egg whites at high speed of an electric mixer until foamy. Gradually add remaining ¼ cup sugar, 1 tablespoon at a time, beating until stiff peaks form. Stir one-fourth of egg white mixture into batter. Fold in remaining egg white mixture.

Pour batter into an ungreased 10-inch tube pan, spreading evenly. Bake at 350° for 35 to 40 minutes or until cake springs back when lightly touched. Invert pan; cool 45 minutes. Loosen cake from sides of pan, using a narrow metal spatula; remove cake from pan. Yield: 10 servings.

PER SERVING: 146 CALORIES (10% FROM FAT)
FAT 1.7G (SATURATED FAT 0.5G)
PROTEIN 3.5G   CARBOHYDRATE 29.0G
CHOLESTEROL 66MG   SODIUM 89MG

FYI

Angel food and sponge cakes depend on beaten egg whites for their light texture. To get the best results, separate the eggs while cold, but let the whites sit at room temperature 20 minutes before beating.

PEPPERMINT CAKE ROLL

11 round peppermint candies, finely crushed
     and divided (about ⅓ cup)
2 cups low-fat vanilla ice cream, softened
Vegetable cooking spray
Basic Sponge Cake batter (page 39)
2 tablespoons powdered sugar, divided

Stir ¼ cup crushed candies into ice cream. Cover and freeze.

Coat a 15- x 10- x 1-inch jellyroll pan with cooking spray, and line with wax paper. Coat wax paper with cooking spray; sprinkle with remaining 2 tablespoons crushed candies.

Spread Basic Sponge Cake batter evenly into prepared pan. Bake at 350° for 15 minutes or until cake springs back when lightly touched in center.

Sift 1 tablespoon powdered sugar in a 15- x 10-inch rectangle onto a towel. When cake is done, immediately loosen from sides of pan, and turn out onto towel; carefully peel off wax paper. Cool cake 1 minute. Starting at narrow end, roll up cake and towel together. Place, seam side down, on a wire rack, and let cool completely (about 1 hour).

Carefully unroll cake; remove towel. Spread cake with ice cream mixture, leaving a ½-inch margin around outside edges. Reroll cake; place, seam side down, on a serving platter. Cover loosely, and freeze until firm.

Let stand at room temperature 10 minutes. Sift remaining 1 tablespoon powdered sugar over cake. To serve, slice cake with a serrated knife. Yield: 10 servings.

PER SERVING: 213 CALORIES (12% FROM FAT)
FAT 2.8G (SATURATED FAT 1.2G)
PROTEIN 4.4G   CARBOHYDRATE 42.8G
CHOLESTEROL 67MG   SODIUM 140MG

Peppermint Cake Roll

PEACH MELBA CAKE ROLL

You may omit the schnapps, if you'd prefer.

1 (12-ounce) package frozen raspberries in
   light syrup, thawed
Vegetable cooking spray
Basic Sponge Cake batter (page 39)
2 tablespoons powdered sugar
1 cup diced fresh ripe peaches
1 cup peach nonfat frozen yogurt, softened
1 tablespoon peach schnapps

Place raspberries in container of an electric blender; cover and process until smooth, stopping twice to scrape down sides. Cover and chill.

Coat a 15- x 10- x 1-inch jellyroll pan with cooking spray. Line pan with wax paper; coat wax paper with cooking spray. Spread Basic Sponge Cake batter into prepared pan. Bake at 350° for 15 minutes or until cake springs back when lightly touched in center.

Sift 2 tablespoons powdered sugar in a 15- x 10-inch rectangle on a towel. When cake is done, immediately loosen from sides of pan, and turn out onto towel; carefully peel off wax paper. Let cake cool 1 minute. Starting at narrow end, roll up cake and towel together. Place, seam side down, on a wire rack; let cool completely (about 1 hour).

Combine peaches, yogurt, and schnapps. Unroll cake, and remove towel. Spread yogurt mixture over cake, leaving a 1-inch margin around edges. Reroll cake; cover and freeze until yogurt mixture is firm. Serve each slice on top of 1 tablespoon plus 2 teaspoons raspberry puree. Yield: 10 servings.

PER SERVING: 217 CALORIES (10% FROM FAT)
FAT 2.3G (SATURATED FAT 0.7G)
PROTEIN 4.5G   CARBOHYDRATE 45.0G
CHOLESTEROL 88MG   SODIUM 120MG

COFFEE ANGEL FOOD CAKE

1 tablespoon instant coffee granules
1 tablespoon hot water
1 (14.5-ounce) package angel food cake mix
1 teaspoon almond extract
1 teaspoon vanilla extract
2 tablespoons instant coffee granules
1 tablespoon hot water
¼ cup plus 2 tablespoons stick margarine,
   softened
1 (16-ounce) package powdered sugar, sifted
3 tablespoons skim milk

Combine 1 tablespoon coffee granules and 1 tablespoon water in a small bowl; stir well, and set aside.

Prepare angel food cake batter according to package directions. Fold in coffee mixture and flavorings. Spoon batter into an ungreased 10-inch tube pan, spreading evenly. Break large air pockets by cutting through batter with a knife. Bake at 375° for 30 minutes or until cake springs back when lightly touched. Invert pan, and let cool for 40 minutes. Loosen cake from sides of pan, using a narrow metal spatula. Invert cake onto a serving plate; set aside to cool completely.

Combine 2 tablespoons coffee granules and 1 tablespoon water in a small bowl; stir well, and set aside. Beat margarine at high speed of an electric mixer until creamy. Add coffee mixture; beat well. Gradually add powdered sugar, beating at medium speed until blended. Add milk; beat well. Spread frosting over top and sides of cake. Store loosely covered in refrigerator. Yield: 12 servings.

PER SERVING: 292 CALORIES (18% FROM FAT)
FAT 5.8G (SATURATED FAT 1.1G)
PROTEIN 2.2G   CARBOHYDRATE 58.3G
CHOLESTEROL 0MG   SODIUM 119MG

Coffee Cheesecake

You may decrease the amount of coffee granules if you prefer less coffee flavor.

Vegetable cooking spray
¾ cup graham cracker crumbs
2 tablespoons sugar
2 tablespoons reduced-calorie stick margarine, melted
1 tablespoon unsweetened cocoa
⅔ cup sugar
⅓ cup all-purpose flour
1 tablespoon cornstarch
1 teaspoon vanilla extract
1 (8-ounce) package Neufchâtel cheese
1 (8-ounce) carton nonfat process cream cheese
2 eggs
½ cup skim milk
2½ tablespoons instant coffee granules
⅓ cup nonfat sour cream
3 egg whites
¼ cup sugar

Coat a 9-inch springform pan with cooking spray. Combine crumbs and next 3 ingredients, and stir well. Firmly press crumb mixture into bottom and 2 inches up sides of pan; set aside.

Combine ⅔ cup sugar and next 6 ingredients in a large bowl; beat at high speed of an electric mixer until smooth. Combine milk and coffee granules; stir well. Add milk mixture and sour cream to cheese mixture; beat until smooth.

Beat egg whites at high speed of an electric mixer until soft peaks form. Add ¼ cup sugar, 1 tablespoon at a time, beating until stiff peaks form. Fold egg white mixture into cheese mixture.

Pour into prepared pan. Bake at 300° for 1 hour or until almost set. Turn oven off; loosen cake from sides of pan, using a narrow metal spatula or knife. Let cheesecake stand in oven with door slightly open for 1 hour. Remove from oven; cover and chill 8 hours. Yield: 12 servings.

Per Serving: 211 Calories (30% from Fat)
Fat 7.0g (Saturated Fat 3.4g)
Protein 8.2g   Carbohydrate 27.8g
Cholesterol 53mg   Sodium 286mg

Marbled Cheesecake

Vegetable cooking spray
½ cup chocolate wafer cookie crumbs (about 8 cookies)
1 cup sugar
¼ cup all-purpose flour
1 tablespoon vanilla extract
1 (8-ounce) carton nonfat process cream cheese, softened
1 (8-ounce) carton light process cream cheese, softened
1 (16-ounce) carton nonfat sour cream
4 eggs
3 ounces sweet baking chocolate, melted

Coat bottom of a 9-inch springform pan with cooking spray; sprinkle with cookie crumbs, and set aside.

Combine sugar and next 5 ingredients in a bowl. Beat at medium speed of an electric mixer until smooth. Add eggs, one at a time; beat well after each addition.

Pour half of cheese mixture into a bowl; add melted chocolate, stirring until well blended. Spoon alternating mounds of plain and chocolate cheese mixtures into prepared pan; swirl with a knife to create a marbled effect.

Bake cheesecake at 300° for 1 hour and 5 minutes or until almost set (center will be soft but will firm when chilled). Turn oven off; let stand in oven with door slightly open for 30 minutes. Remove from oven; let cool on a wire rack. Cover and chill at least 2 hours. Yield: 12 servings.

Per Serving: 269 Calories (32% from Fat)
Fat 9.7g (Saturated Fat 4.5g)
Protein 10.5g   Carbohydrate 35.7g
Cholesterol 97mg   Sodium 317mg

Strawberry-Amaretto Cheesecake

STRAWBERRY-AMARETTO CHEESECAKE

Vegetable cooking spray
¼ cup amaretti cookie crumbs (about 28 small
    cookies) or graham cracker crumbs
1 (24-ounce) carton 1% low-fat cottage cheese
2 (8-ounce) cartons light process cream cheese
1 cup plus 1 tablespoon sugar, divided
2 tablespoons amaretto
2 eggs
4 egg whites
⅛ teaspoon cream of tartar
2¾ cups halved fresh strawberries, divided

Coat the bottom of a 10-inch springform pan with cooking spray; sprinkle with crumbs, and set aside.

Position knife blade in food processor bowl; add cheeses, and process until smooth. Add ¾ cup sugar, amaretto, and 2 eggs; process until smooth. Pour into a large bowl; set aside.

Beat 4 egg whites and cream of tartar at high speed of an electric mixer until foamy. Gradually add ¼ cup sugar, 1 tablespoon at a time, beating until stiff peaks form. Gently stir one-fourth of egg white mixture into cheese mixture. Gently fold in remaining egg white mixture.

Pour mixture into prepared pan. Bake at 325° for 50 minutes. Remove pan from oven. Cool on a wire rack 1 hour. Cover and chill at least 8 hours.

Combine ¾ cup strawberries and 1 tablespoon sugar in food processor bowl; process until smooth. Arrange remaining 2 cups strawberries on top of cheesecake. Drizzle with strawberry glaze. Yield: 14 servings.

Note: Substitute 2 tablespoons skim milk plus ½ teaspoon almond extract for amaretto, if desired.

PER SERVING: 232 CALORIES (33% FROM FAT)
FAT 8.6G (SATURATED FAT 4.2G)
PROTEIN 11.8G   CARBOHYDRATE 27.0G
CHOLESTEROL 52MG   SODIUM 438MG

COOKIE JAR DELIGHTS

*L*et your children experience the fun of sneaking into the kitchen to grab a fresh, home-baked cookie from the cookie jar. And why not? Low in fat and calories, the cookies in this chapter are treats you can feel good about.

First try Ginger Cookies (page 50), declared by the "kids" in our test kitchen to be some of the best. You'll be slipping in some extra nutrition from oats and raisins when you stock the jar with Oatmeal-Raisin Cookies (page 49).

Try Peanut Butter Swirl Brownies (page 56) when you have a few minutes for yourself. Enjoy one with a glass of cold milk, and you'll feel like a child again, too.

Clockwise from top: *Peppermint Spritz Cookies (recipe on page 53), Butter-Nut Sugar Cookies (recipe on page 51), Apricot Lace Cookies (recipe on page 46), and Mocha Meringues (recipe on page 54)*

APRICOT LACE COOKIES

(pictured on page 44)

2   cups quick-cooking oats, uncooked
1   cup sugar
1   cup firmly packed light brown sugar
¼   cup all-purpose flour
½   cup stick margarine, melted
½   teaspoon almond extract
2   eggs, beaten
Vegetable cooking spray
½   cup plus 2 teaspoons no-sugar-added apricot
     or raspberry spread
1   (1-ounce) square semisweet chocolate

Combine first 4 ingredients in a bowl, and stir well. Add margarine, almond extract, and eggs, stirring well. Drop by level teaspoonfuls, 2 inches apart, onto cookie sheets coated with cooking spray. Bake at 350° for 7 minutes or until edges are lightly browned. Let stand 4 minutes; remove from sheets, and place on wire racks. Let cookies cool completely.

Place ½ teaspoon fruit spread on bottoms of half the cookies; top with remaining cookies. Arrange cookies in a single layer on wire racks.

Place chocolate in a heavy-duty, zip-top plastic bag; seal bag. Submerge in boiling water until chocolate melts. Snip a tiny hole in end of bag; drizzle chocolate over the cookies. Freeze 10 minutes. Yield: 52 cookies.

PER COOKIE: 71 CALORIES (29% FROM FAT)
FAT 2.3G (SATURATED FAT 0.6G)
PROTEIN 0.9G   CARBOHYDRATE 12.1G
CHOLESTEROL 9MG   SODIUM 27MG

OLD-FASHIONED HERMITS

⅓   cup stick margarine, softened
¾   cup firmly packed brown sugar
¼   cup frozen egg substitute, thawed
½   teaspoon lemon extract
¼   teaspoon vanilla extract
1½   cups all-purpose flour
1½   teaspoons baking powder
½   teaspoon ground allspice
½   teaspoon ground cinnamon
¼   teaspoon ground cloves
¼   teaspoon ground nutmeg
¼   cup unsweetened apple juice
Vegetable cooking spray
60   raisins (about ¼ cup)

Beat margarine at medium speed of an electric mixer until creamy; gradually add brown sugar, beating until well blended. Add egg substitute and flavorings; beat well.

Combine flour and next 5 ingredients, stirring well. Add to creamed mixture alternately with apple juice, beginning and ending with flour mixture. Mix well after each addition.

Drop dough by rounded teaspoonfuls, 2 inches apart, onto cookie sheets coated with cooking spray. Press a raisin in center of each cookie. Bake at 325° for 15 to 17 minutes or until lightly browned. Cool slightly on cookie sheets. Remove from cookie sheets, and cool completely on wire racks. Yield: 5 dozen.

PER COOKIE: 33 CALORIES (30% FROM FAT)
FAT 1.1G (SATURATED FAT 0.2G)
PROTEIN 0.4G   CARBOHYDRATE 5.5G
CHOLESTEROL 0MG   SODIUM 22MG

FYI

Whether the recipe calls for regular or reduced-calorie margarine, be sure to use the stick type. Do not use a spread or whipped margarine for cookies—these contain water, which will result in a wetter dough than desired.

Old-Fashioned Hermits and Chocolate Chip Cookies

CHOCOLATE CHIP COOKIES

3½ tablespoons brown sugar
3 tablespoons light-colored corn syrup
1½ tablespoons stick margarine
½ teaspoon vanilla extract
2 egg whites
2 tablespoons water
⅔ cup all-purpose flour
½ cup instant nonfat dry milk powder
½ teaspoon baking soda
¼ teaspoon salt
1 cup quick-cooking oats, uncooked
½ cup semisweet chocolate mini-morsels
Vegetable cooking spray

Combine first 4 ingredients in a medium bowl; beat at medium speed of an electric mixer until light and fluffy. Add egg whites and water; beat well.

Combine flour, dry milk powder, soda, and salt in a medium bowl, stirring well. Gradually add flour mixture to creamed mixture, mixing well. Stir in oats and chocolate mini-morsels.

Drop dough by level tablespoonfuls, 2 inches apart, onto cookie sheets coated with cooking spray. Bake at 375° for 9 to 11 minutes or until lightly browned. Cool slightly on cookie sheets. Remove from cookie sheets, and cool completely on wire racks. Yield: 2 dozen.

PER COOKIE: 73 CALORIES (28% FROM FAT)
FAT 2.3G (SATURATED FAT 0.9G)
PROTEIN 2.2G   CARBOHYDRATE 11.2G
CHOLESTEROL 1MG   SODIUM 72MG

CHOCOLATE PEPPERMINT COOKIES

½ cup stick margarine, softened
½ cup sugar
½ cup firmly packed brown sugar
½ cup frozen egg substitute, thawed
1 teaspoon vanilla extract
2¼ cups all-purpose flour
1 teaspoon baking powder
¾ teaspoon baking soda
¼ teaspoon salt
¼ cup plus 1 tablespoon unsweetened cocoa
⅔ cup finely crushed round peppermint
    candies (about 30 candies)
Vegetable cooking spray

Beat margarine at medium speed of an electric mixer until creamy; gradually add sugars, beating well. Add egg substitute and vanilla; beat well.

Combine flour and next 4 ingredients. Add to margarine mixture, stirring just until blended. Stir in crushed candy. Drop dough by level tablespoonfuls, 2 inches apart, onto cookie sheets coated with cooking spray. Bake at 350° for 10 to 12 minutes. Remove from cookie sheets, and let cool on wire racks. Yield: 44 cookies.

PER COOKIE: 75 CALORIES (26% FROM FAT)
FAT 2.2G (SATURATED FAT 0.5G)
PROTEIN 1.1G   CARBOHYDRATE 12.9G
CHOLESTEROL 0MG   SODIUM 66MG

Chocolate Peppermint Cookies

Oatmeal-Raisin Cookies

OATMEAL-RAISIN COOKIES

¾ cup firmly packed brown sugar
¼ cup plus 2 tablespoons stick margarine,
  softened
¼ cup sugar
1 egg
¼ cup plus 2 tablespoons skim milk
1 teaspoon vanilla extract
1½ cups all-purpose flour
¾ teaspoon baking soda
½ teaspoon ground cinnamon
¼ teaspoon salt
¼ teaspoon ground nutmeg
1½ cups quick-cooking oats, uncooked
¾ cup raisins
Vegetable cooking spray

Beat first 3 ingredients at medium speed of an electric mixer until light and fluffy. Add egg; beat well. Add milk and vanilla; beat well.

Combine flour and next 4 ingredients; gradually add to creamed mixture, beating well. Stir in oats and raisins.

Drop dough by rounded tablespoonfuls onto cookie sheets coated with cooking spray. Bake at 375° for 9 minutes or until lightly browned. Cool on wire racks. Yield: 4 dozen.

PER COOKIE: 66 CALORIES (26% FROM FAT)
FAT 1.9G (SATURATED FAT 0.4G)
PROTEIN 1.1G   CARBOHYDRATE 11.5G
CHOLESTEROL 5MG   SODIUM 49MG

Ginger Cookies

GINGER COOKIES

¼ cup plus 2 tablespoons stick margarine,
   softened
⅔ cup plus 3 tablespoons sugar, divided
¼ cup molasses
1 egg
2 cups all-purpose flour
2 teaspoons baking soda
1 teaspoon ground ginger
1 teaspoon ground cinnamon
½ teaspoon ground mace
Vegetable cooking spray

Beat margarine at medium speed of an electric mixer until creamy; gradually add ⅔ cup sugar, beating until light and fluffy. Add molasses and egg; beat well.

Combine flour and next 4 ingredients; gradually add to creamed mixture, stirring until well blended. Divide dough in half; wrap each portion in plastic wrap, and freeze 30 minutes.

Shape each portion of dough into 26 (1-inch) balls, and roll in remaining 3 tablespoons sugar. Place 2 inches apart on cookie sheets coated with cooking spray. Bake at 350° for 12 minutes or until lightly browned. Remove from cookie sheets; cool on wire racks. Store in an airtight container. Yield: 52 cookies.

PER COOKIE: 46 CALORIES (29% FROM FAT)
FAT 1.5G (SATURATED FAT 0.3G)
PROTEIN 0.6G   CARBOHYDRATE 7.7G
CHOLESTEROL 4MG   SODIUM 49MG

BUTTER-NUT SUGAR COOKIES

(pictured on page 44)

Vanilla, butter, and nut flavoring can be found among other extracts and flavorings in most larger supermarkets.

1 cup plus 2 tablespoons firmly packed brown sugar
3 ounces Neufchâtel cheese (about ⅓ cup)
¼ cup plus 2 tablespoons stick margarine, softened
2 tablespoons skim milk
½ teaspoon vanilla, butter, and nut flavoring
1 egg
3 cups all-purpose flour
1½ teaspoons baking powder
½ teaspoon salt
Vegetable cooking spray
½ cup sifted powdered sugar
1½ teaspoons water
Food coloring (optional)

Beat first 3 ingredients at medium speed of an electric mixer until light and fluffy. Add milk, flavoring, and egg, and beat well. Combine flour, baking powder, and salt. Add to creamed mixture, beating well.

Divide dough into 4 equal portions. Working with one portion of dough at a time, roll to ⅛-inch thickness on a well-floured surface; cover and chill remaining dough.

Cut dough with a 2-inch decorative cookie cutter; place cookies, 1 inch apart, on cookie sheets coated with cooking spray. Bake at 350° for 10 minutes; remove from cookie sheets, and let cool on wire racks. Repeat procedure with remaining dough.

Combine powdered sugar, water, and food coloring, if desired; stir well. Spoon into a decorating bag fitted with a small, round tip; pipe onto cookies. Yield: 8 dozen.

PER COOKIE: 33 CALORIES (27% FROM FAT)
FAT 1.0G (SATURATED FAT 0.3G)
PROTEIN 0.6G CARBOHYDRATE 5.3G
CHOLESTEROL 3MG SODIUM 26MG

VANILLA SLICE-AND-BAKE COOKIES

⅓ cup stick margarine, softened
⅔ cup sugar
¼ cup frozen egg substitute, thawed
2 teaspoons vanilla extract
2 cups plus 1 tablespoon all-purpose flour
½ teaspoon baking soda
¼ teaspoon salt
¾ cup crisp rice cereal
Vegetable cooking spray

Beat margarine at medium speed of an electric mixer until creamy; gradually add sugar, beating until light and fluffy. Add egg substitute and vanilla; beat well.

Combine flour, soda, and salt. Gradually add flour mixture to creamed mixture; mix well. Stir in cereal.

Divide dough into 2 equal portions; place each portion on a sheet of plastic wrap, and shape into an 8- x 1½-inch log. Wrap logs in plastic wrap, and freeze until firm.

Unwrap logs, and cut into ¼-inch slices. Place slices, 1 inch apart, on cookie sheets coated with cooking spray. Bake at 350° for 6 to 8 minutes or until lightly browned. Remove from cookie sheets, and let cool on wire racks. Yield: 64 cookies.

PER COOKIE: 32 CALORIES (28% FROM FAT)
FAT 1.0G (SATURATED FAT 0.2G)
PROTEIN 0.5G CARBOHYDRATE 5.2G
CHOLESTEROL 0MG SODIUM 30MG

Quick Tip

Rather than wait for margarine to soften, unwrap and place on a microwave-safe plate. Just pop the plate into the microwave oven, and microwave at LOW (10% power) for 30 seconds or more until softened.

Peanut Butter and Jelly Sandwich Cookies

PEANUT BUTTER AND JELLY SANDWICH COOKIES

⅓ cup reduced-calorie stick margarine, softened
¼ cup creamy peanut butter
¾ cup granulated brown sugar
¼ cup frozen egg substitute, thawed
1 teaspoon vanilla extract
1¾ cups all-purpose flour
½ teaspoon baking soda
½ cup plus 1½ tablespoons grape jelly or strawberry jam

Beat margarine and peanut butter at medium speed of an electric mixer until fluffy; gradually add sugar, and beat well. Add egg substitute and vanilla; beat well.

Combine flour and soda in a small bowl, stirring well. Gradually add flour mixture to creamed mixture, mixing well.

Shape dough into 56 (1-inch) balls. Place balls, 2 inches apart, on ungreased cookie sheets; flatten cookies in a crisscross pattern with a fork. Bake at 350° for 9 minutes or until lightly browned. Cool slightly on cookie sheets. Remove from cookie sheets; cool completely on wire racks.

Place about 1 teaspoon jelly on bottoms of half the cooled cookies; top with remaining cookies. Yield: 28 cookies.

PER COOKIE: 88 CALORIES (27% FROM FAT)
FAT 2.6G (SATURATED FAT 0.4G)
PROTEIN 1.7G   CARBOHYDRATE 14.9G
CHOLESTEROL 0MG   SODIUM 52MG

PEPPERMINT SPRITZ COOKIES

(pictured on page 44)

¾ cup plus 2 tablespoons sugar
¼ cup plus 2 tablespoons stick margarine, softened
3 ounces Neufchâtel cheese (about ⅓ cup)
¼ cup skim milk
1 teaspoon peppermint extract
1 egg
3 cups all-purpose flour
2 teaspoons baking powder
½ teaspoon salt
Vegetable cooking spray
1 cup sifted powdered sugar
1 tablespoon plus 1 teaspoon skim milk
⅛ teaspoon peppermint extract
14 round peppermint candies, finely crushed

Beat sugar, margarine, and cheese at medium speed of an electric mixer until light and fluffy. Add ¼ cup milk, 1 teaspoon peppermint extract, and egg; beat well.

Combine flour, baking powder, and salt; gradually add to creamed mixture, stirring well.

Press dough through a cookie press fitted with a 1-inch-long serrated disk, following the manufacturer's instructions; make long strips on cookie sheets coated with cooking spray. Cut each strip into 3-inch pieces. Bake at 350° for 12 minutes or until lightly browned. Cool cookies completely on wire racks.

Combine powdered sugar, 1 tablespoon plus 1 teaspoon milk, and ⅛ teaspoon peppermint extract; stir well. Brush one-third of each cookie with powdered sugar mixture, and sprinkle with crushed candies. Yield: 5½ dozen.

PER COOKIE: 58 CALORIES (23% FROM FAT)
FAT 1.5G (SATURATED FAT 0.4G)
PROTEIN 0.9G   CARBOHYDRATE 10.4G
CHOLESTEROL 4MG   SODIUM 37MG

SNICKERDOODLES

¾ cup reduced-calorie stick margarine,
   softened
1½ cups sugar
2 eggs
1 teaspoon vanilla extract
4 cups all-purpose flour
1 teaspoon baking soda
½ teaspoon salt
2 teaspoons cream of tartar
2 tablespoons sugar
1½ teaspoons ground cinnamon
Vegetable cooking spray

Beat margarine at medium speed of an electric mixer until fluffy; gradually add 1½ cups sugar, beating well. Add eggs and vanilla; beat well.

Combine flour and next 3 ingredients in a bowl, stirring well. Gradually add flour mixture to creamed mixture, mixing well. Cover and chill 2 hours.

Combine 2 tablespoons sugar and cinnamon in a small bowl; set aside.

Shape dough into 1-inch balls; roll balls in sugar mixture. Place balls, 2 inches apart, on cookie sheets coated with cooking spray. Bake at 400° for 8 minutes or until cookies are very lightly browned. Cool slightly on cookie sheets. Remove from cookie sheets, and cool completely on wire racks. Yield: 6 dozen.

PER COOKIE: 55 CALORIES (23% FROM FAT)
FAT 1.4G (SATURATED FAT 0.2G)
PROTEIN 0.9G   CARBOHYDRATE 9.9G
CHOLESTEROL 6MG   SODIUM 54MG

Did You Know?

The popularity of Snickerdoodles goes all the way back to 19th-century New England. Typically, the cookie dough is sprinkled with or rolled in a cinnamon-sugar mixture and develops a cracked surface during baking.

MOCHA MERINGUES

(pictured on page 44)

Be sure not to make these delicate cookies on a rainy day—the extra moisture can cause meringues to become soft and sticky.

6 egg whites
¾ teaspoon cream of tartar
¾ cup sugar
1½ teaspoons instant coffee granules, crushed
¾ ounce semisweet chocolate, grated

Cover 3 large cookie sheets with parchment paper. Draw 60 (2½- x 1-inch) rectangles, 1 inch apart, on paper. Turn paper over to avoid contact with lead. Secure paper to cookie sheets with masking tape, and set aside.

Beat egg whites and cream of tartar at high speed of an electric mixer until foamy. Gradually add sugar, 1 tablespoon at a time, beating until stiff peaks form. (Do not underbeat.) Gently fold coffee granules and chocolate into meringue.

Spoon meringue mixture into a pastry bag fitted with a No. 8 (½-inch) round tip. Starting at one corner of an outlined rectangle, pipe meringue mixture in spiral fashion down long side of rectangle; repeat procedure down other long side of rectangle. (Spiral sides should touch in center, forming a solid base and ¼-inch-high sides for each rectangle.) Repeat procedure for remaining rectangles.

Bake at 200° for 1½ hours or until dry. Turn oven off, and let meringues cool in closed oven at least 1 hour. Carefully remove meringues from paper. Store in an airtight container up to 3 weeks. Yield: 5 dozen.

PER COOKIE: 13 CALORIES (7% FROM FAT)
FAT 0.1G (SATURATED FAT 0.1G)
PROTEIN 0.4G   CARBOHYDRATE 2.8G
CHOLESTEROL 0MG   SODIUM 5MG

DUTCH ALMOND BARS

1½ cups all-purpose flour
¼ teaspoon baking powder
⅛ teaspoon salt
1 teaspoon ground cinnamon
¼ cup sugar
2½ tablespoons stick margarine, chilled
1 tablespoon ice water
1 egg, lightly beaten
Vegetable cooking spray
1 egg white, lightly beaten
2 tablespoons sugar
2 tablespoons sliced almonds

Combine first 5 ingredients in a large bowl. Cut in chilled margarine with a pastry blender until mixture resembles coarse meal. Stir in ice water and beaten egg. Turn dough out onto a surface; knead into a ball.

Press dough into the bottom of a 9-inch square pan coated with cooking spray. Brush with egg white; sprinkle with 2 tablespoons sugar and almonds.

Bake at 375° for 15 minutes or until edges are lightly browned. Cut into bars; cool completely in pan on a wire rack. Yield: 2 dozen.

PER BAR: 60 CALORIES (29% FROM FAT)
FAT 1.9G (SATURATED FAT 0.3G)
PROTEIN 1.4G   CARBOHYDRATE 9.4G
CHOLESTEROL 9MG   SODIUM 31MG

APPLE CRUNCH BARS

2 cups all-purpose flour
1 cup firmly packed brown sugar
¼ cup stick margarine, softened
1 teaspoon baking soda
⅛ teaspoon salt
1 teaspoon ground cinnamon
¼ teaspoon ground nutmeg
1 teaspoon vanilla extract
1 (8-ounce) carton plain low-fat yogurt
1 egg
2 cups peeled, chopped Granny Smith apple
Vegetable cooking spray
¼ cup chopped walnuts

Combine first 3 ingredients in a bowl, beating well at medium speed of an electric mixer.

Reserve 2 cups flour mixture, and set aside. Add soda and next 3 ingredients to remaining flour mixture; beat well. Add vanilla, yogurt, and egg; beat well. Stir in apple.

Press reserved 2 cups flour mixture into the bottom of a 13- x 9- x 2-inch pan coated with cooking spray. Sprinkle walnuts over flour mixture. Spread apple mixture over prepared crust. Bake at 350° for 40 minutes or until browned. Cool completely in pan on a wire rack. Cut into bars. Yield: 2 dozen.

PER BAR: 110 CALORIES (25% FROM FAT)
FAT 3.1G (SATURATED FAT 0.6G)
PROTEIN 2.1G   CARBOHYDRATE 18.6G
CHOLESTEROL 9MG   SODIUM 81MG

CHOCOLATE CHIP BARS

¼ cup plus 2 tablespoons stick margarine,
   softened
⅓ cup sugar
¾ cup firmly packed dark brown sugar
2 egg whites
2 teaspoons vanilla extract
2½ cups all-purpose flour
½ teaspoon baking soda
⅛ teaspoon salt
½ cup semisweet chocolate mini-morsels
Vegetable cooking spray

Beat margarine and sugars at medium speed of an electric mixer until light and fluffy. Add egg whites and vanilla; beat well.

Combine flour, soda, and salt; gradually add to creamed mixture, beating well. Stir in chocolate morsels.

Press cookie dough into the bottom of a 13- x 9- x 2-inch pan coated with cooking spray. Bake at 375° for 10 minutes. Cool in pan on a wire rack. Cut into bars. Yield: 4 dozen.

PER BAR: 67 CALORIES (30% FROM FAT)
FAT 2.2G (SATURATED FAT 0.7G)
PROTEIN 0.9G   CARBOHYDRATE 11.0G
CHOLESTEROL 0MG   SODIUM 35MG

FROSTED CHOCOLATE BROWNIES

½ cup plus 3 tablespoons reduced-calorie stick margarine, softened
1⅓ cups sugar
8 egg whites
½ cup nonfat sour cream
⅓ cup evaporated skimmed milk
2 teaspoons vanilla extract
1⅓ cups all-purpose flour
1 teaspoon baking powder
½ teaspoon salt
⅔ cup unsweetened cocoa
Vegetable cooking spray
Creamy Chocolate Frosting (page 25)

Beat margarine at medium speed of an electric mixer until creamy; gradually add sugar, and beat well. Add egg whites, sour cream, evaporated milk, and vanilla; beat well.

Combine flour and next 3 ingredients in a small bowl; stir well. Add flour mixture to creamed mixture, mixing well. Pour batter into a 13- x 9- x 2-inch pan coated with cooking spray. Bake at 350° for 25 minutes or until a wooden pick inserted in center comes out clean. Cool in pan on a wire rack. Spread Creamy Chocolate Frosting over cooled brownies; cut into squares. Yield: 2 dozen.

PER BROWNIE: 183 CALORIES (19% FROM FAT)
FAT 3.9G (SATURATED FAT 0.8G)
PROTEIN 3.5G   CARBOHYDRATE 34.1G
CHOLESTEROL 0MG   SODIUM 164MG

PEPPERMINT BROWNIES

Reduce vanilla extract to 1 teaspoon, and add ½ teaspoon peppermint extract. Sprinkle 3 tablespoons finely crushed round peppermint candies over frosted brownies.

PER BROWNIE: 185 CALORIES (18% FROM FAT)
FAT 3.6G (SATURATED FAT 0.7G)
PROTEIN 3.4G   CARBOHYDRATE 25.6G
CHOLESTEROL 0MG   SODIUM 110MG

PEANUT BUTTER SWIRL BROWNIES

¼ cup plus 2 tablespoons reduced-calorie stick margarine, melted
1¼ cups firmly packed brown sugar
½ cup frozen egg substitute, thawed
1 teaspoon vanilla extract
1½ cups all-purpose flour
½ teaspoon baking powder
½ teaspoon salt
2 tablespoons unsweetened cocoa
¼ cup 25% less-fat creamy peanut butter
Vegetable cooking spray

Combine margarine and sugar in a medium bowl; add egg substitute. Beat well at medium speed of an electric mixer. Add vanilla; beat well.

Combine flour, baking powder, and salt; add to sugar mixture, stirring well.

Divide batter in half. Stir cocoa into one half; stir peanut butter into other half. (Peanut butter mixture will be thick.)

Spoon dollops of each batter alternately into a 9-inch square pan coated with cooking spray. Cut through batters in pan with a knife to create a swirled pattern. Bake at 350° for 25 minutes or until a wooden pick inserted in center comes out clean. Remove from oven, and let cool completely on a wire rack. Cut into squares. Yield: 16 brownies.

PER BROWNIE: 162 CALORIES (25% FROM FAT)
FAT 4.5G (SATURATED FAT 0.7G)
PROTEIN 3.2G   CARBOHYDRATE 28.1G
CHOLESTEROL 0MG   SODIUM 151MG

Quick Tip

Measure dry ingredients before moist ones to minimize cleanup. Having two sets of measuring cups will enable you to measure consecutive ingredients without stopping to wash out the measure repeatedly.

Peanut Butter Swirl Brownies

GLAZED OATMEAL-SPICE BLONDIES

1½ cups quick-cooking oats, uncooked
1 cup all-purpose flour
½ teaspoon baking soda
1 teaspoon ground ginger
1 teaspoon ground cinnamon
⅛ teaspoon ground cloves
¾ cup firmly packed brown sugar
¾ cup pitted dates
½ cup boiling water
¼ cup stick margarine
2 teaspoons vanilla extract
2 egg whites
1 egg
Vegetable cooking spray
1 cup sifted powdered sugar
2 tablespoons water

Combine first 6 ingredients. Stir well; set aside.

Position knife blade in food processor bowl; add brown sugar and dates, and process until dates are finely chopped. Add boiling water and margarine, and process until smooth. Add vanilla, egg whites, and egg, and process until well blended. Add date mixture to oat mixture; stir well.

Pour batter into a 13- x 9- x 2-inch pan coated with cooking spray. Bake at 375° for 18 minutes or until a wooden pick inserted in the center comes out clean. Cool in pan on wire rack 5 minutes. Combine powdered sugar and 2 tablespoons water. Spread over top; cool. Cut into bars. Yield: 2½ dozen.

PER BAR: 97 CALORIES (19% FROM FAT)
FAT 2.0G (SATURATED FAT 0.4G)
PROTEIN 1.6G   CARBOHYDRATE 18.5G
CHOLESTEROL 7MG   SODIUM 40MG

TART LEMON SQUARES

1 cup all-purpose flour
⅓ cup sifted powdered sugar
¼ cup plus 1 tablespoon chilled stick
    margarine, cut into small pieces
Vegetable cooking spray
1 cup sugar
2 tablespoons all-purpose flour
1½ teaspoons grated lemon rind
½ teaspoon baking powder
¼ teaspoon salt
3 egg whites
1 egg
¼ cup plus 3 tablespoons fresh lemon juice
¼ teaspoon butter flavoring
2 tablespoons powdered sugar

Combine 1 cup flour and ⅓ cup powdered sugar in a bowl; cut in margarine with a pastry blender until mixture resembles coarse meal.

Press mixture firmly and evenly into the bottom of an 11- x 7- x 1½-inch baking dish coated with cooking spray. Bake at 350° for 20 minutes or until lightly browned.

Combine sugar and next 6 ingredients in a medium bowl; stir with a wire whisk until blended. Stir in lemon juice and butter flavoring. Pour mixture over prepared crust. Bake at 350° for 20 minutes or until set. Cool completely on a wire rack. Cut into squares. Sift 2 tablespoons powdered sugar over squares. Yield: 2 dozen.

PER SQUARE: 89 CALORIES (27% FROM FAT)
FAT 2.7G (SATURATED FAT 0.5G)
PROTEIN 1.3G   CARBOHYDRATE 15.2G
CHOLESTEROL 9MG   SODIUM 68MG

Microwave Magic

Lemons are easier to squeeze and yield more juice if they are at room temperature. If they have been refrigerated, heat 1 lemon at a time in the microwave at HIGH for 20 to 40 seconds or just until warm to the touch. Roll firmly on the countertop to soften.

Tart Lemon Squares

FANCIFUL FRUIT

For an easy, low-fat dessert, nothing beats fresh fruit. Slice it and serve with cheese, or cut it up to toss with honey and mint for a simple ambrosia.

But fruit can be elegant too. Strawberry-Filled Meringues (page 68) is a sophisticated dessert that is as visually delightful as it is delicious. Poached Pears with Raspberry Sherbet (page 72), although easy to prepare, is another show-stopper to serve for formal occasions.

If it's comfort food you want, serve fruit atop slightly sweetened shortcakes or cooked in a crisp or crumble.

Champagne Fruit Compote (recipe on page 62)

CHAMPAGNE FRUIT COMPOTE

(pictured on page 60)

¾ cup unsweetened white grape juice
1 tablespoon honey
1 teaspoon grated orange rind
4 (3-inch) sticks cinnamon
2 cups fresh strawberries, halved and divided
3 medium-size ripe nectarines, sliced
1 cup seedless green grapes
1 cup seedless red grapes
3 kiwifruit, peeled and thinly sliced
½ cup champagne or sparkling white grape juice, chilled

Combine first 4 ingredients in a small saucepan. Bring to a boil; reduce heat, and simmer 5 minutes. Remove and discard cinnamon sticks. Cover and chill thoroughly.

Place 1 cup strawberries in a large glass bowl. Layer nectarines and grapes over strawberries; top with remaining 1 cup strawberries and kiwifruit. Cover and chill thoroughly.

To serve, stir champagne into chilled grape juice mixture; pour over fruit. Yield: 6 (1-cup) servings.

PER SERVING: 154 CALORIES (6% FROM FAT)
FAT 1.0G (SATURATED FAT 0.2G)
PROTEIN 1.8G   CARBOHYDRATE 34.0G
CHOLESTEROL 0MG   SODIUM 4MG

HONEYED AMBROSIA

½ cup honey
¼ cup chopped fresh mint
¼ cup lemon juice
3 cups fresh grapefruit sections
4 oranges, peeled and thinly sliced
3 tablespoons flaked coconut, toasted

Combine honey, mint, and lemon juice in a small bowl; stir well.

Combine grapefruit sections and orange slices in a medium bowl. Drizzle honey mixture over fruit;

toss gently to coat. Cover and chill at least 2 hours. Just before serving, sprinkle fruit mixture with coconut. Yield: 6 (1-cup) servings.

PER SERVING: 182 CALORIES (6% FROM FAT)
FAT 1.2G (SATURATED FAT 1.0G)
PROTEIN 1.8G   CARBOHYDRATE 45.2G
CHOLESTEROL 0MG   SODIUM 10MG

AMBROSIA PARFAITS

1 (16-ounce) carton vanilla low-fat yogurt
¼ cup crushed pineapple in juice, drained
1 banana, peeled and sliced
1 (11-ounce) can mandarin oranges in light syrup, drained
1 tablespoon flaked coconut, toasted
4 strawberries, sliced

Spoon yogurt onto several layers of heavy-duty paper towels; spread to ½-inch thickness. Cover with additional paper towels; let stand 5 minutes. Scrape yogurt into a bowl, using a rubber spatula. Add pineapple, and stir well.

Spoon 2 tablespoons yogurt mixture into each of 4 (6-ounce) parfait glasses; top evenly with banana slices. Spoon 2 tablespoons yogurt mixture over each banana layer; top with orange segments.

Dollop remaining yogurt mixture evenly over orange segments; sprinkle with coconut. Top with sliced strawberries. Yield: 4 servings.

PER SERVING: 190 CALORIES (14% FROM FAT)
FAT 2.9G (SATURATED FAT 2.1G)
PROTEIN 6.2G   CARBOHYDRATE 36.4G
CHOLESTEROL 6MG   SODIUM 87MG

FYI

Speed up the ripening process of fresh fruit by placing it in a loosely closed paper bag. Store the bag at room temperature until the fruit is ripe.

Ambrosia Parfaits

BANANAS MELBA

1 (12-ounce) package frozen unsweetened
   raspberries, thawed
¼ cup sugar
¼ cup unsweetened orange juice
1 tablespoon cornstarch
1⅓ cups low-fat vanilla ice cream
2 medium bananas, peeled and sliced

   Place raspberries in container of an electric
blender or food processor; cover and process 45 seconds or until smooth. Transfer to a wire-mesh
strainer; press with back of spoon against the sides
of the strainer to squeeze out juice. Discard seeds
and pulp in strainer.
   Combine raspberry juice and next 3 ingredients
in a saucepan. Cook over medium heat, stirring
constantly, until thickened. Remove from heat.
   Set aside ¼ cup of raspberry sauce. Spoon the
remaining raspberry sauce evenly into 4 individual
dessert bowls. Scoop ⅓ cup ice cream into each
bowl. Arrange banana slices evenly around ice
cream. Drizzle 1 tablespoon reserved sauce over
each serving. Serve immediately. Yield: 4 servings.

PER SERVING: 204 CALORIES (11% FROM FAT)
FAT 2.5G (SATURATED FAT 1.3G)
PROTEIN 2.9G   CARBOHYDRATE 45.8G
CHOLESTEROL 6MG   SODIUM 38MG

MAPLE-RUM BANANA SUNDAE

6 small, firm, ripe bananas (about 1¾ pounds)
⅓ cup maple syrup
¼ cup dark rum
1 teaspoon margarine
2 cups low-fat vanilla ice cream
2 tablespoons chopped pecans, toasted

Maple-Rum Banana Sundae

Peel bananas. Cut bananas in half crosswise and then lengthwise; set aside.

Combine maple syrup, rum, and margarine in a large skillet; bring to a simmer. Add bananas; cook 30 seconds. Turn bananas over, and cook an additional 30 seconds. Arrange 4 banana pieces on each of 6 dessert plates; top each with ⅓ cup ice cream, 1 tablespoon sauce, and 1 teaspoon pecans. Yield: 6 servings.

PER SERVING: 202 CALORIES (20% FROM FAT)
FAT 4.6G (SATURATED FAT 1.6G)
PROTEIN 2.7G CARBOHYDRATE 40.6G
CHOLESTEROL 6MG SODIUM 47MG

TROPICAL FRUIT BOWLS

1 tablespoon cornstarch
Dash of ground cinnamon
½ cup unsweetened pineapple juice
½ cup unsweetened pineapple tidbits
1 tablespoon low-sugar orange marmalade
1 medium cantaloupe, peeled, quartered, and
    seeded
2 cups vanilla nonfat frozen yogurt
1 tablespoon plus 1 teaspoon flaked coconut

Combine first 3 ingredients in a small saucepan; stir well. Bring to a boil over medium heat, and cook, stirring constantly, 1 minute or until thickened. Remove from heat; add pineapple tidbits and marmalade, stirring well. Let cool completely.

Place 1 cantaloupe wedge in each of 4 serving bowls; top each with ½ cup frozen yogurt and ¼ cup pineapple sauce. Sprinkle each with 1 teaspoon coconut. Serve immediately. Yield: 4 servings.

PER SERVING: 183 CALORIES (5% FROM FAT)
FAT 1.1G (SATURATED FAT 0.8G)
PROTEIN 4.9G CARBOHYDRATE 41.4G
CHOLESTEROL 0MG SODIUM 79MG

FRESH FRUIT MÉLANGE WITH STRAWBERRY SAUCE

2 fresh ripe peaches, peeled and sliced
2 tablespoons lemon juice
Strawberry Sauce
2 cups diced fresh pineapple
2 medium kiwifruit, peeled and cut into ¼-inch
    slices
1 cup fresh strawberries, halved

Combine peaches and lemon juice in a small bowl; toss gently.

Spoon Strawberry Sauce evenly onto 6 individual dessert plates. Arrange peaches, pineapple, kiwifruit, and strawberries evenly over sauce. Serve immediately. Yield: 6 servings.

STRAWBERRY SAUCE
2 cups fresh strawberries
2 tablespoons sugar
¼ cup red currant jelly

Position knife blade in food processor bowl; add strawberries and sugar. Process 1 to 2 minutes or until smooth; set aside.

Melt jelly in a saucepan over medium heat, stirring constantly. Add strawberry mixture, stirring well. Cover and chill thoroughly. Yield: 1⅔ cups.

PER SERVING: 135 CALORIES (5% FROM FAT)
FAT 0.7G (SATURATED FAT 0.1G)
PROTEIN 1.3G CARBOHYDRATE 33.5G
CHOLESTEROL 0MG SODIUM 3MG

Quick Tip

To peel fresh peaches, submerge them in boiling water for 30 seconds and then immediately plunge them into cold water. The loosened skins will slip off easily.

CHOCOLATE CRÊPES WITH TROPICAL FRUIT

½ cup all-purpose flour
1 tablespoon sugar
1 tablespoon unsweetened cocoa
½ cup evaporated skimmed milk
1 egg
1 tablespoon reduced-calorie margarine,
    melted
Vegetable cooking spray
⅔ cup chopped fresh pineapple
½ cup chopped fresh papaya
2 medium kiwifruit, peeled and sliced
Chocolate Glaze
2 tablespoons sliced almonds, toasted

Combine first 6 ingredients in container of an electric blender; cover and process until smooth. Chill batter at least 2 hours.

Coat a 6-inch crêpe pan or nonstick skillet with cooking spray; place over medium heat until just hot, not smoking. Pour 2 tablespoons batter into pan; quickly tilt pan in all directions so batter covers pan in a thin film. Cook 1 minute or until crêpe can be shaken loose. Flip crêpe, and cook about 30 seconds.

Place crêpes on a towel to cool. Stack crêpes between layers of wax paper to prevent sticking. Repeat procedure until all batter is used.

Arrange pineapple, papaya, and kiwifruit down center of each crêpe, placed spotted side up. Roll up crêpes, and place seam side down on individual dessert plates; drizzle each crêpe with 1 tablespoon Chocolate Glaze. Sprinkle evenly with almonds. Yield: 8 servings.

CHOCOLATE GLAZE
2 tablespoons reduced-calorie margarine
2 tablespoons unsweetened cocoa
2 tablespoons water
½ teaspoon vanilla extract
1 cup sifted powdered sugar

Melt margarine in a small saucepan. Add cocoa and water, stirring until smooth. Cook over medium-low heat, stirring constantly, until mixture begins to thicken (do not boil). Remove saucepan from heat, and add vanilla and powdered sugar, stirring until smooth. Yield: ½ cup.

PER SERVING: 177 CALORIES (25% FROM FAT)
FAT 4.9G (SATURATED FAT 0.9G)
PROTEIN 4.1G   CARBOHYDRATE 30.3G
CHOLESTEROL 28MG   SODIUM 70MG

MINTED STRAWBERRIES IN TULIP CUPS

2 tablespoons brown sugar
1 tablespoon plus 1 teaspoon honey
2 teaspoons stick margarine
¼ cup all-purpose flour
⅛ teaspoon ground cinnamon
¼ teaspoon vanilla extract
Vegetable cooking spray
2 cups sliced fresh strawberries (about 1 pint)
1½ teaspoons powdered sugar
1 teaspoon finely chopped fresh mint
Fresh mint sprigs (optional)

Combine first 3 ingredients in a saucepan; bring to a boil over medium-high heat. Remove from heat; stir in flour, cinnamon, and vanilla.

Working quickly, spoon batter evenly into 4 circles onto a cookie sheet coated with cooking spray. Using fingers, pat batter into 4½-inch circles. Bake at 325° for 10 minutes or until golden. Let stand 30 seconds; immediately remove cookies from pan, and place each cookie over an inverted 6-ounce custard cup. Shape cookies around cups to form tulip-shaped cups; let cool completely.

Combine strawberries, powdered sugar, and chopped mint; toss gently. Cover and chill.

To serve, spoon ½ cup chilled strawberry mixture into each tulip-shaped cookie cup. Garnish with fresh mint sprigs, if desired. Yield: 4 servings.

PER SERVING: 112 CALORIES (19% FROM FAT)
FAT 2.4G (SATURATED FAT 0.4G)
PROTEIN 1.3G   CARBOHYDRATE 22.5G
CHOLESTEROL 0MG   SODIUM 25MG

Minted Strawberries in Tulip Cups

STRAWBERRY-FILLED MERINGUES

Try not to make meringues when it's rainy or humid, for the moisture can make them sticky.

6 egg whites
¾ teaspoon cream of tartar
¾ cup superfine sugar
¾ teaspoon vanilla extract
¼ teaspoon almond extract
Glazed Strawberry Filling

The peaks of stiffly beaten egg whites should just hold their shape and not fall over.

Line 2 baking sheets with parchment paper. Draw 4 (4-inch) circles on each sheet of paper; turn paper over to avoid contact with lead. Set aside.

Beat egg whites and cream of tartar at high speed of an electric mixer until soft peaks form. Gradually add sugar, 1 tablespoon at a time, beating until stiff peaks form. Gently fold in flavorings.

Spoon meringue into a decorating bag fitted with a large star tip. Pipe meringue onto circles on paper, building up sides to form a shell; fill in bottom. Bake at 225° for 1 hour and 20 minutes. Turn oven off. Cool completely in oven at least 2 hours or overnight with oven door closed. (Empty baked meringue shells may be stored in an airtight container for up to 3 days.)

To serve, fill shells with Glazed Strawberry Filling. Yield: 8 servings.

Pipe a circle with the meringue; then fill in the circle to form the bottom of the shell.

GLAZED STRAWBERRY FILLING

3 cups fresh strawberry halves
2 tablespoons sugar
1 (10-ounce) package frozen raspberries in light syrup, thawed
2 teaspoons cornstarch
2 teaspoons Cointreau or other orange-flavored liqueur
1½ teaspoons lemon juice

Combine strawberry halves and sugar, tossing gently. Set aside.

Place raspberries in container of an electric blender or food processor; cover and process until smooth. Press raspberries through a sieve; set puree aside, and discard seeds.

Combine strained raspberries and cornstarch in a small saucepan; stir until smooth. Bring to a boil over medium heat, stirring constantly, and cook 1 minute or until mixture is thickened. Remove sauce from heat; stir in liqueur and lemon juice.

Pour raspberry sauce over strawberry halves; toss gently to coat. Cover and chill 2 to 3 hours. Toss gently before spooning into baked meringue shells. Yield: 2½ cups.

Note: To make superfine sugar, place granulated sugar in an electric blender; process until finely ground.

PER SERVING: 157 CALORIES (2% FROM FAT)
FAT 0.3G (SATURATED FAT 0.0G)
PROTEIN 3.1G   CARBOHYDRATE 36.3G
CHOLESTEROL 0MG   SODIUM 60MG

Strawberry-Filled Meringues

Vanilla Truffle Torte

VANILLA TRUFFLE TORTE

6 egg whites
½ teaspoon cream of tartar
¾ cup sugar
1½ cups 1% low-fat milk
1 (3-inch) piece vanilla bean, split lengthwise
½ cup sugar
3 tablespoons cornstarch
2 tablespoons water
½ cup vanilla milk morsels
¼ cup plus 3 tablespoons nonfat process
    cream cheese
2 cups sliced fresh strawberries, divided
1 tablespoon powdered sugar

Cover baking sheets with parchment paper. Draw 3 (9-inch) circles on paper. Turn paper over to avoid contact with lead. Secure with masking tape, and set aside.

Beat egg whites and cream of tartar in a large bowl at high speed of an electric mixer until foamy. Gradually add ¾ cup sugar, 1 tablespoon at a time, beating until stiff peaks form. (Do not underbeat.)

Using the back of a spoon, spread one-third of egg white mixture into each circle on baking sheets. Bake at 200° for 3 hours or until dry. Turn oven off; let meringues cool in closed oven at least 12 hours. Remove meringues from paper.

Pour milk into a saucepan. Scrape seeds from vanilla bean; add seeds and bean to milk. Cook over medium-low heat 20 minutes, stirring occasionally. Remove from heat; discard vanilla bean.

Combine ½ cup sugar and cornstarch in a small bowl. Gradually add water, stirring with a wire whisk until blended; add to milk. Bring to a boil over medium heat, and cook 1 minute, stirring constantly. Reduce heat to low, and add vanilla milk morsels and cream cheese; cook, stirring constantly, 1 minute or until melted. Pour into a bowl; cover surface of mixture with plastic wrap, and chill thoroughly.

Place 1 meringue on a serving platter; spread with half of cream cheese mixture. Arrange half of strawberries over cream cheese mixture. Place another meringue over strawberries; spread evenly with remaining cream cheese mixture. Arrange the remaining strawberries over cream cheese; place remaining meringue over strawberries. Sprinkle powdered sugar over top. Serve immediately. Yield: 8 servings.

PER SERVING: 247 CALORIES (14% FROM FAT)
FAT 3.9G (SATURATED FAT 2.2G)
PROTEIN 6.9G   CARBOHYDRATE 47.0G
CHOLESTEROL 4MG   SODIUM 171MG

ORANGES IN CARAMEL SAUCE

¾ cup sugar
⅔ cup water
1 cup warm water
5 medium navel oranges (about 3 pounds)
¼ cup plus 1 tablespoon chopped pistachios

Combine sugar and ⅔ cup water in a small, heavy saucepan. Place over medium heat, and cook 40 minutes or until golden, stirring occasionally. Remove from heat, and *slowly* add 1 cup warm water without stirring. (Add the water slowly to prevent the hot sugar mixture from splattering.) Place over medium heat; stir well. Cook 3 minutes or until sugar melts. Pour caramel sauce into a bowl; cover and chill 1 hour.

Use a vegetable peeler to remove rind from 1 orange; cut rind into thin strips. Cook in boiling water 1 minute; drain. Plunge into cold water, and drain again. Set aside. Peel oranges, and make 6 crosswise cuts in each orange to within ½ inch of opposite side. Arrange oranges, cut sides up, in a shallow dish. Pour caramel sauce over oranges; cover and marinate in refrigerator at least 1 hour.

To serve, place 1 orange in each of 5 dessert compotes. Drizzle each with ¼ cup sauce, and top with orange rind strips and 1 tablespoon pistachios. Yield: 5 servings.

PER SERVING: 224 CALORIES (16% FROM FAT)
FAT 4.0G (SATURATED FAT 0.5G)
PROTEIN 2.9G   CARBOHYDRATE 47.8G
CHOLESTEROL 0MG   SODIUM 1MG

COCONUT APPLES WITH CARAMEL SAUCE

Apples that cook without falling apart are a must in this recipe—Golden Delicious and Rome Beauty apples work well.

2 tablespoons chopped pecans
4 soft commercial coconut macaroons, broken into small pieces
2 large Golden Delicious apples (about 1¾ pounds), each peeled, cored, and cut into 6 wedges
1 egg, lightly beaten
Vegetable cooking spray
½ cup caramel-flavored topping
3 tablespoons apple cider
1 tablespoon bourbon or additional apple cider
¾ cup vanilla low-fat frozen yogurt

Position knife blade in food processor bowl; add pecans and macaroon pieces, and process 10 seconds or until finely chopped. Dip apple wedges into egg, and dredge in macaroon mixture. Place apples on a baking sheet coated with cooking spray. Bake at 375° for 35 minutes or until apples are browned and tender.

Combine caramel topping, apple cider, and bourbon in a small bowl; stir well with a wire whisk. Spoon 2 tablespoons caramel sauce onto each of 6 dessert plates, and top with 2 apple wedges and 2 tablespoons frozen yogurt. Yield: 6 servings.

PER SERVING: 291 CALORIES (19% FROM FAT)
FAT 6.2G (SATURATED FAT 2.8G)
PROTEIN 3.5G   CARBOHYDRATE 57.9G
CHOLESTEROL 38MG   SODIUM 119MG

POACHED PEARS WITH RASPBERRY SHERBET

Bartlett, Anjou, and Bosc pears are recommended for poaching. Cooking times can vary according to the ripeness of the fruit.

3 large ripe pears
2 teaspoons lemon juice
1 cup white Zinfandel or other blush wine
½ cup sugar
½ cup unsweetened apple juice
1 tablespoon lemon juice
1 (1-ounce) square semisweet chocolate, melted
1½ cups raspberry sherbet
Fresh raspberries (optional)
Fresh mint sprigs (optional)

Peel and core pears; cut in half lengthwise, and brush with 2 teaspoons lemon juice.

Combine wine and next 3 ingredients in a large saucepan; bring to a boil. Add pears; cover, reduce heat, and simmer 15 minutes or until tender, turning once. Transfer pears and poaching liquid to a bowl; cover and chill thoroughly.

Drizzle half of chocolate onto 6 dessert plates. Transfer pears to plates, using a slotted spoon. Discard poaching liquid. Top each pear with ¼ cup sherbet. Drizzle remaining chocolate over sherbet. If desired, garnish with fresh raspberries and mint. Serve immediately. Yield: 6 servings.

PER SERVING: 133 CALORIES (16% FROM FAT)
FAT 2.3G (SATURATED FAT 1.0G)
PROTEIN 1.1G   CARBOHYDRATE 29.9G
CHOLESTEROL 0MG   SODIUM 34MG

Did You Know?

Refrigerating fruit stops its natural ripening process. Bananas, cantaloupe, peaches, and pears will ripen after they are picked and should be refrigerated after becoming fully ripe. Other fruits like berries, cherries, and grapes are ripe upon picking and should be refrigerated immediately.

Poached Pears with Raspberry Sherbet

Peaches-and-Honey Shortcakes

PEACHES-AND-HONEY SHORTCAKES

1¼ cups lemon low-fat yogurt
3 tablespoons light brown sugar
2 tablespoons low-fat sour cream
4 cups peeled, sliced fresh peaches (about 1½ pounds)
3 tablespoons honey
2¾ cups all-purpose flour
1 tablespoon plus 1 teaspoon baking powder
½ teaspoon salt
¾ teaspoon ground cinnamon
2 tablespoons light brown sugar
¼ cup plus 1 tablespoon chilled stick margarine, cut into small pieces
1 cup skim milk
Vegetable cooking spray

Combine lemon yogurt, 3 tablespoons brown sugar, and sour cream in a bowl; stir well. Cover and chill yogurt mixture at least 30 minutes.

Combine peaches and honey in a large bowl; toss gently, and set aside.

Combine flour and next 4 ingredients in a bowl; cut in margarine with a pastry blender until mixture resembles coarse meal. Add milk; stir just until dry ingredients are moistened.

Turn dough out onto a lightly floured surface; knead 4 or 5 times. Roll dough to ½-inch thickness; cut with a 3-inch biscuit cutter. Place on a baking sheet coated with cooking spray. Bake at 450° for 9 minutes or until golden.

To serve, split biscuits; top each with ⅓ cup peach mixture and 2 tablespoons yogurt mixture. Yield: 12 servings.

PER SERVING: 249 CALORIES (21% FROM FAT)
FAT 5.7G (SATURATED FAT 1.2G)
PROTEIN 5.2G   CARBOHYDRATE 45.3G
CHOLESTEROL 1MG   SODIUM 283MG

APPLE CRISP WITH MACADAMIA NUTS

¼ cup all-purpose flour
¼ cup sugar
¼ cup firmly packed brown sugar
2 tablespoons chopped macadamia nuts
⅛ teaspoon ground cinnamon
2½ tablespoons chilled stick margarine, cut into small pieces
5 cups thinly sliced peeled Rome apple
Vegetable cooking spray
2 tablespoons apricot preserves

Combine first 5 ingredients in a bowl; stir well. Cut in margarine with a pastry blender until mixture resembles coarse meal; set aside.

Place apple slices in an 8-inch square baking dish coated with cooking spray; drop apricot preserves, by teaspoonfuls, onto apple slices, and sprinkle evenly with the flour mixture. Bake at 375° for 35 minutes or until bubbly and golden. Yield: 6 (¾-cup) servings.

PER SERVING: 216 CALORIES (30% FROM FAT)
FAT 7.3G (SATURATED FAT 1.3G)
PROTEIN 0.9G   CARBOHYDRATE 39.2G
CHOLESTEROL 0MG   SODIUM 62MG

BLUEBERRY PEACH CRUMBLE

6 commercial coconut macaroons
½ cup all-purpose flour
¼ cup sugar, divided
2 tablespoons brown sugar
3 tablespoons reduced-calorie stick margarine, melted
3 cups sliced fresh peaches
3 cups fresh blueberries
1 tablespoon all-purpose flour
2¼ cups vanilla nonfat frozen yogurt

Place macaroons on a baking sheet. Bake at 275° for 25 minutes.

Position knife blade in food processor bowl; add macaroons, and process until coarsely chopped. Combine chopped macaroons, ½ cup flour, 2 tablespoons sugar, and brown sugar in a medium bowl. Add margarine, and stir well. Set aside.

Combine peaches and blueberries in an 8-inch square baking dish. Combine remaining 2 tablespoons sugar and 1 tablespoon flour; sprinkle over fruit mixture. Top with macaroon mixture. Bake, uncovered, at 350° for 30 minutes. Serve warm, and top each serving with ¼ cup frozen yogurt. Yield: 9 servings.

PER SERVING: 240 CALORIES (27% FROM FAT)
FAT 7.1G (SATURATED FAT 0.4G)
PROTEIN 3.8G   CARBOHYDRATE 43.2G
CHOLESTEROL 0MG   SODIUM 75MG

TROPICAL FRUIT CRISP

½ cup all-purpose flour
⅓ cup quick-cooking oats, uncooked
3 tablespoons brown sugar
2 tablespoons chopped pistachios, toasted
½ teaspoon ground cardamom
3 tablespoons reduced-calorie stick margarine
2 cups cubed fresh pineapple
1 medium mango, peeled, seeded, and cubed
1 medium papaya, peeled, seeded, and cubed
2 tablespoons sugar
2 teaspoons quick-cooking tapioca, uncooked
¼ teaspoon ground nutmeg

Combine first 5 ingredients in a small bowl; cut in margarine with a pastry blender until mixture resembles coarse meal. Set aside.

Combine pineapple, mango, and papaya in an 8-inch square baking dish. Sprinkle sugar, tapioca, and nutmeg evenly over fruit; toss well. Sprinkle flour mixture evenly over fruit mixture. Bake at 350° for 25 minutes or until crust is golden and fruit is bubbly. Yield: 8 servings.

PER SERVING: 147 CALORIES (26% FROM FAT)
FAT 4.3G (SATURATED FAT 0.6G)
PROTEIN 2.2G   CARBOHYDRATE 26.8G
CHOLESTEROL 0MG   SODIUM 45MG

Pear Charlotte

Place whole pear slice in bottom of prepared soufflé dish.

Line sides and bottom of dish with bread; fill with pear mixture.

With scissors, trim tops of bread halves even with pear mixture.

Arrange bread slice and trimmed tops over pear mixture. Cover with foil.

PEAR CHARLOTTE

Vegetable cooking spray
1 unpeeled Bartlett or Anjou pear
8 (½-ounce) very thin slices white bread
3½ pounds very ripe Bartlett or Anjou pears
2 teaspoons margarine
⅓ cup firmly packed dark brown sugar
1½ tablespoons lemon juice
¼ teaspoon ground cinnamon
¾ cup vanilla nonfat frozen yogurt, softened

Coat a 1-quart glass soufflé dish with cooking spray; line bottom of dish with wax paper. Cut 1 unpeeled pear in half lengthwise. Cut a ⅛-inch slice from one of pear halves; place in dish.

Trim crusts from bread; discard crusts. Cut one bread slice into small cubes; set aside. Cut 5 bread slices in half lengthwise. Standing bread slices vertically in dish, line sides with 10 bread halves. Place 1 bread slice in bottom of dish; arrange bread cubes tightly around whole bread slice.

Peel and core remaining pears; cut lengthwise into slices to equal 8 cups, and set aside.

Melt margarine in a large skillet over medium heat. Stir in sugar, lemon juice, and cinnamon. Add pears; stir gently. Cover and cook pears 15 minutes; stir occasionally. Uncover and cook pears an additional 15 minutes. Drain pears, reserving liquid.

Spoon pear mixture into dish; press firmly with the back of a spoon. With scissors, trim tops of bread halves even with pears; reserve trimmed bread tops. Dip remaining whole bread slice and reserved trimmed bread tops in reserved pear liquid; arrange in center of dish over pears. Cover bread completely with aluminum foil, and cut 6 (1-inch) slits in foil. Bake at 350° for 50 minutes or until lightly browned. Uncover and cool in dish 1 hour on a wire rack.

To serve, loosen edges of charlotte with a knife; invert charlotte onto serving plate, and cut into wedges. Combine yogurt and ¼ cup plus 2 tablespoons reserved pear cooking liquid; serve with charlotte. Yield: 6 servings.

PER SERVING: 262 CALORIES (10% FROM FAT)
FAT 2.9G (SATURATED FAT 0.4G)
PROTEIN 3.5G   CARBOHYDRATE 59.9G
CHOLESTEROL 1MG   SODIUM 131MG

FREEZER FAVORITES

A bowl of homemade ice cream on a hot summer afternoon is a refreshing treat. But if the thought of the traditional ingredients of cream, eggs, and sugar is more oppressive than the weather, you've come to the right place. Here's a delightful collection of frozen yogurts, sorbets, sherbets, and ice milks—perfect low-fat refreshment for summer or even year round.

Also included are a couple of simple recipes for freezer pops (page 81). The kids can help make them, and they will certainly help eat them. Raspberry Bombe (page 92), a fancier dessert, is great for entertaining, especially since it can be prepared well ahead of time and kept in the freezer until needed.

Apple-Cranberry Ice and Peach Sherbet (recipes on pages 86 and 89)

Banana-Chocolate Chip Pops and Honey-Banana Pops

BANANA-CHOCOLATE CHIP POPS

1 (8-ounce) carton coffee-flavored low-fat
   yogurt
1 cup 1% low-fat chocolate milk
2 small bananas, peeled and cut into chunks
3 tablespoons semisweet chocolate mini-
   morsels
8 (3-ounce) paper cups
8 wooden sticks

Combine first 3 ingredients in container of an electric blender or food processor; cover and process until smooth.

Stir in chocolate morsels. Pour mixture evenly into paper cups. Cover tops of cups with aluminum foil, and insert a stick through foil into center of each cup. Freeze at least 4 hours.

To serve, remove foil, and peel paper cup away from each pop. Yield: 8 pops.

PER POP: 108 CALORIES (27% FROM FAT)
FAT 3.2G (SATURATED FAT 1.5G)
PROTEIN 3.3G   CARBOHYDRATE 18.0G
CHOLESTEROL 1MG   SODIUM 50MG

HONEY-BANANA POPS

2 (8-ounce) cartons vanilla low-fat yogurt
2 medium-size ripe bananas, peeled and
   mashed
2 tablespoons honey
1 teaspoon vanilla extract
¼ teaspoon ground cinnamon
8 (3-ounce) paper cups
8 wooden sticks

Combine first 5 ingredients in container of an electric blender or food processor; cover and process just until smooth.

Pour mixture evenly into paper cups. Cover tops of cups with aluminum foil, and insert a stick through foil into center of each cup. Freeze at least 4 hours.

To serve, remove foil, and peel paper away from each pop. Yield: 8 pops.

PER POP: 91 CALORIES (8% FROM FAT)
FAT 0.8G (SATURATED FAT 0.5G)
PROTEIN 3.1G   CARBOHYDRATE 18.7G
CHOLESTEROL 3MG   SODIUM 38MG

FYI

What does it mean to let a frozen dessert "ripen"? The frozen yogurts, sherbets, and ice milks on pages 82 through 91 may be somewhat soft after the freezing is completed. The process of ripening hardens the mixture and allows flavors to blend.

To ripen, remove the dasher, and scrape the frozen dessert from the dasher into the can. Stir the mixture lightly to blend soft portions with the firmer portions. Cover the can with aluminum foil, and replace the lid.

Pack the freezer bucket with ice and salt, using a higher ratio of salt to ice than for freezing. Cover the freezer with heavy towels or newspaper, and let it stand 1 to 2 hours. Drain off the brine occasionally, and add more ice and salt as needed.

An easy, less traditional way to ripen a frozen dessert is to simply spoon the frozen mixture into freezer-safe containers. Stir lightly, and then cover and freeze the dessert for 1 to 2 hours before eating.

CHOCOLATE FROZEN YOGURT

½ cup sugar
1 tablespoon cornstarch
1½ cups skim milk
1 egg, lightly beaten
½ cup chocolate-flavored syrup
¼ cup light-colored corn syrup
1½ cups plain low-fat yogurt
½ teaspoon vanilla extract

Combine sugar and cornstarch in a saucepan; gradually stir in milk and egg. Bring to a boil, stirring constantly with a wire whisk. Cook, stirring constantly, 1 minute or until mixture is thickened and coats a metal spoon. Remove from heat; stir in syrups. Pour into a bowl; let cool completely. Stir in yogurt and vanilla. Cover and chill 8 hours.

Pour mixture into freezer can of a 1- or 2-quart hand-turned or electric freezer. Freeze according to manufacturer's instructions. Let ripen 1 hour. Yield: 8 (½-cup) servings.

PER SERVING: 184 CALORIES (8% FROM FAT)
FAT 1.6G (SATURATED FAT 0.7G)
PROTEIN 5.2G   CARBOHYDRATE 37.2G
CHOLESTEROL 31MG   SODIUM 87MG

PEACH FROZEN YOGURT

½ cup sugar
1 teaspoon unflavored gelatin
⅛ teaspoon ground nutmeg
½ cup skim milk
2 tablespoons light-colored corn syrup
1½ pounds fresh peaches, peeled and
    quartered
1 cup plain low-fat yogurt
½ teaspoon vanilla extract

Combine first 3 ingredients in a saucepan. Stir in milk; let stand 1 minute. Cook over low heat, stirring until gelatin dissolves, about 5 minutes. Remove from heat; stir in syrup. Let cool.

Position knife blade in food processor bowl; add peaches. Process until smooth, scraping sides of processor bowl occasionally. Combine peach puree, gelatin mixture, yogurt, and vanilla in a large bowl; stir well. Cover and chill 8 hours.

Pour mixture into freezer can of a 2-quart hand-turned or electric freezer. Freeze according to manufacturer's instructions. Let ripen 1 hour. Yield: 10 (½-cup) servings.

PER SERVING: 91 CALORIES (4% FROM FAT)
FAT 0.4G (SATURATED FAT 0.3)
PROTEIN 2.2G   CARBOHYDRATE 20.3G
CHOLESTEROL 2MG   SODIUM 28MG

VANILLA FROZEN YOGURT

½ large vanilla bean, split
2¼ cups skim milk
½ cup sugar
1 envelope unflavored gelatin
Dash of salt
1½ cups plain low-fat yogurt
¼ cup light-colored corn syrup
Fresh mint sprigs (optional)

Scrape seeds from bean. Combine seeds, bean, and milk in a saucepan. Bring to a boil; remove from heat, and let stand 30 minutes. Discard bean.

Add sugar, gelatin, and salt. Let stand 1 minute. Cook over low heat, stirring until gelatin dissolves, about 5 minutes. Let cool completely. Stir in yogurt and corn syrup. Pour into a bowl; cover and chill 8 hours.

Pour mixture into freezer can of a 1- or 2-quart hand-turned or electric freezer. Freeze according to manufacturer's instructions. Let ripen 1 hour. Garnish with mint, if desired. Yield: 8 (½-cup) servings.

Note: Substitute 1 teaspoon vanilla extract for the vanilla bean, if desired. Add to cooled mixture with yogurt and corn syrup.

PER SERVING: 132 CALORIES (5% FROM FAT)
FAT 0.8G (SATURATED FAT 0.5G)
PROTEIN 5.3G   CARBOHYDRATE 26.3G
CHOLESTEROL 4MG   SODIUM 98MG

Clockwise from top left: *Chocolate Frozen Yogurt, Peach Frozen Yogurt, and Vanilla Frozen Yogurt*

Raspberry-Lemon Frozen Yogurt and Cantaloupe Sorbet

Raspberry-Lemon Frozen Yogurt

1 envelope unflavored gelatin
¼ cup cold water
2 (8-ounce) cartons plain nonfat yogurt
1 (10-ounce) package frozen raspberries in
    light syrup, thawed and drained
1 (6-ounce) can frozen lemonade concentrate,
    thawed and undiluted
¾ cup cold water
⅓ cup sugar
Fresh raspberries (optional)
Fresh mint sprigs (optional)

Sprinkle gelatin over ¼ cup cold water in a small saucepan; let stand 1 minute. Cook over low heat, stirring until gelatin dissolves, about 2 minutes.

Combine gelatin mixture, yogurt, and next 4 ingredients in container of an electric blender; cover and process until mixture is smooth, stopping once to scrape down sides.

Pour mixture into freezer can of a 2-quart hand-turned or electric freezer. Freeze according to manufacturer's instructions. Let ripen 1 hour. If desired, garnish with fresh raspberries and mint. Yield: 12 (½-cup) servings.

PER SERVING: 84 CALORIES (1% FROM FAT)
FAT 0.1G (SATURATED FAT 0.1G)
PROTEIN 2.8G   CARBOHYDRATE 18.5G
CHOLESTEROL 1MG   SODIUM 30MG

Very Berry Sorbet

2 cups fresh raspberries
2 cups fresh strawberries, sliced
½ cup sugar
1½ cups sparkling white grape juice
Fresh raspberries (optional)
Fresh strawberries (optional)
Fresh mint sprigs (optional)

Place 2 cups raspberries in a wire-mesh strainer; press raspberries with back of spoon against the sides of the strainer to squeeze out juice. Discard pulp and seeds remaining in strainer.

Combine raspberry juice, 2 cups strawberries, and sugar in container of an electric blender; cover and process until smooth, stopping once to scrape down sides. Combine fruit puree and white grape juice; stir well.

Pour mixture into freezer can of a 2-quart hand-turned or electric freezer. Freeze according to manufacturer's instructions. Let ripen 1 hour. If desired, garnish with fresh raspberries, strawberries, and mint sprigs. Yield: 10 (½-cup) servings.

PER SERVING: 83 CALORIES (3% FROM FAT)
FAT 0.3G (SATURATED FAT 0.0G)
PROTEIN 0.6G   CARBOHYDRATE 20.6G
CHOLESTEROL 0MG   SODIUM 2MG

Cantaloupe Sorbet

½ cup sugar
½ cup water
2 teaspoons grated lemon rind
9 cups cubed cantaloupe (about 2 medium)
¼ cup fresh lemon juice
Additional cubed cantaloupe (optional)
Fresh mint sprigs (optional)

Combine first 3 ingredients in a small saucepan. Bring to a boil; cook over medium heat, stirring constantly, until sugar dissolves. Remove from heat, and let cool slightly.

Position knife blade in food processor bowl; add 9 cups cantaloupe. Process until smooth. Transfer to a large bowl; add sugar mixture and lemon juice, stirring well. Cover and chill thoroughly.

Pour mixture into freezer can of a 2-quart hand-turned or electric freezer. Freeze according to manufacturer's instructions. Let ripen 1 hour. If desired, garnish with additional cantaloupe and mint. Yield: 12 (½-cup) servings.

PER SERVING: 75 CALORIES (4% FROM FAT)
FAT 0.3G (SATURATED FAT 0.2G)
PROTEIN 1.1G   CARBOHYDRATE 18.6G
CHOLESTEROL 0MG   SODIUM 11MG

APPLE-CRANBERRY ICE

(pictured on page 78)

3 cups water, divided
1½ cups fresh cranberries
¾ cup sugar, divided
⅔ cup unsweetened apple juice
2 tablespoons lemon juice

Combine ½ cup water, cranberries, and ¼ cup sugar in a nonaluminum saucepan. Bring to a boil over medium heat; cook 8 minutes or until cranberries pop, stirring frequently. Remove from heat, and let cool.

Position knife blade in food processor bowl. Add cranberry mixture; process until smooth. Strain puree through a sieve; discard pulp.

Combine remaining 2½ cups water, remaining ½ cup sugar, cranberry puree, apple juice, and lemon juice in a bowl, stirring well; cover and chill.

Pour cranberry mixture into freezer can of a 2-quart hand-turned or electric freezer. Freeze according to manufacturer's instructions. Let ripen 1 hour. Yield: 8 (½-cup) servings.

PER SERVING: 92 CALORIES (1% FROM FAT)
FAT 0.1G (SATURATED FAT 0.0G)
PROTEIN 0.1G   CARBOHYDRATE 23.9G
CHOLESTEROL 0MG   SODIUM 1MG

HEAVENLY LEMON SHERBET

When removing the lemon rind, be careful not to remove any of the white pith underneath or your sherbet will taste bitter.

1 lemon
1 cup sugar
3 cups 2% low-fat milk
½ cup fresh lemon juice
½ cup water
⅛ teaspoon salt

Using a vegetable peeler, carefully remove rind from lemon.

Position knife blade in a food processor bowl, and add rind and sugar; process until rind is minced. Spoon sugar mixture into a bowl. Add milk and remaining ingredients; stir well.

Pour mixture into freezer can of a 2-quart or 1-gallon hand-turned or electric freezer, and freeze according to manufacturer's instructions. Let ripen at least 1 hour. Yield: 11 (½-cup) servings.

PER SERVING: 108 CALORIES (11% FROM FAT)
FAT 1.3G (SATURATED FAT 0.8G)
PROTEIN 2.4G   CARBOHYDRATE 23.4G
CHOLESTEROL 5MG   SODIUM 60MG

REFRESHING LIME SHERBET

¼ cup plain nonfat yogurt
¼ cup nonfat cottage cheese
1½ cups sugar
3½ cups water
1 teaspoon grated lime rind
½ cup fresh lime juice
1 drop green food coloring (optional)
Lime wedges (optional)
Edible flowers (optional)

Combine yogurt and cottage cheese in container of an electric blender; cover and process until smooth. Set aside.

Combine sugar, water, and grated lime rind in a medium saucepan; bring to a boil. Cover, reduce heat, and simmer 10 minutes. Remove from heat, and stir in lime juice. Let mixture cool to room temperature.

Combine yogurt mixture and lime mixture in a bowl, stirring well. Stir in green food coloring, if desired. Pour lime mixture into freezer can of a 2-quart hand-turned or electric freezer. Freeze according to manufacturer's instructions. Let ripen 1 hour. If desired, garnish with lime wedges and edible flowers. Yield: 10 (½-cup) servings.

PER SERVING: 126 CALORIES (0% FROM FAT)
FAT 0.0G (SATURATED FAT 0.0G)
PROTEIN 1.1G   CARBOHYDRATE 31.7G
CHOLESTEROL 0MG   SODIUM 26MG

Refreshing Lime Sherbet

Frozen Rainbow Torte

FROZEN RAINBOW TORTE

Make your own lime sherbet with the recipe on page 86, or use commercial sherbet.

1 cup gingersnap crumbs (about 30 cookies)
2 tablespoons reduced-calorie stick margarine, melted
Vegetable cooking spray
1 quart lime sherbet, softened
1 (15¾-ounce) can crushed pineapple in juice, drained
1 quart orange sherbet, softened
1 quart raspberry sherbet, softened
1 (10-ounce) package frozen raspberries in light syrup, thawed and drained
Fresh raspberries (optional)
Fresh mint sprigs (optional)

Combine gingersnap crumbs and margarine. Press crumb mixture firmly over bottom of a 10-inch springform pan coated with cooking spray.

Combine lime sherbet and pineapple in a large bowl, stirring well; spread over crumb crust. Cover and freeze until firm.

Spread orange sherbet over frozen lime sherbet mixture. Cover and freeze until firm.

Combine raspberry sherbet and thawed raspberries in a large bowl, stirring well; spread over orange sherbet. Cover and freeze at least 8 hours.

To serve, quickly dip base of pan in warm water to loosen crust from pan; carefully remove sides of pan. If desired, garnish with raspberries and mint sprigs. Slice into wedges. Serve immediately. Yield: 16 servings.

PER SERVING: 228 CALORIES (15% FROM FAT)
FAT 3.8G (SATURATED FAT 1.6G)
PROTEIN 2.0G   CARBOHYDRATE 35.6G
CHOLESTEROL 5MG   SODIUM 111MG

PEACH SHERBET

(pictured on page 78)

1 (8-ounce) carton plain low-fat yogurt
½ cup unsweetened orange juice
⅓ cup honey
2 cups peeled, sliced ripe peaches or 2 cups frozen unsweetened peaches, partially thawed

Position knife blade in food processor bowl; add all ingredients. Process until peaches are finely chopped. Pour mixture into an 8-inch square pan; freeze until almost firm.

Break mixture into large pieces, and place in processor bowl. Process several seconds or until fluffy but not thawed. Return mixture to pan and freeze until firm. Let stand at room temperature 10 minutes before serving. Yield: 6 (½-cup) servings.

PER SERVING: 111 CALORIES (5% FROM FAT)
FAT 0.6G (SATURATED FAT 0.4G)
PROTEIN 2.5G   CARBOHYDRATE 25.6G
CHOLESTEROL 2MG   SODIUM 28MG

PINEAPPLE SHERBET

¾ cup sugar
4 cups low-fat buttermilk
2 teaspoons vanilla extract
1 (20-ounce) can unsweetened crushed pineapple, undrained

Combine all ingredients in a large bowl, and stir well. Position knife blade in food processor bowl; add half of pineapple mixture, and pulse 3 times. Pour mixture into freezer can of a 2-quart hand-turned or electric freezer.

Repeat procedure with remaining pineapple mixture, and freeze according to manufacturer's instructions. Let ripen at least 1 hour. Yield: 12 (½-cup) servings.

PER SERVING: 119 CALORIES (11% FROM FAT)
FAT 1.4G (SATURATED FAT 0.9G)
PROTEIN 3.2G   CARBOHYDRATE 24.1G
CHOLESTEROL 0MG   SODIUM 42MG

VANILLA ICE MILK

Don't worry about not cooking the egg substitute in this and other frozen desserts—it has been pasteurized during processing and is safe to eat without additional heating.

2 cups 2% low-fat milk, divided
1 vanilla bean, split lengthwise
1 cup evaporated skimmed milk
¾ cup sugar
¾ cup frozen egg substitute, thawed

Pour 1 cup low-fat milk into a small saucepan. Scrape seeds from vanilla bean; add seeds and bean to milk. Cook over low heat 20 minutes. Remove from heat; discard vanilla bean. Pour milk mixture into a bowl; cover and chill.

Combine evaporated milk, sugar, egg substitute, remaining 1 cup low-fat milk, and chilled milk mixture in a bowl. Stir with a wire whisk until well blended.

Pour mixture into freezer can of a 2-quart hand-turned or electric freezer, and freeze according to manufacturer's instructions. Let ripen at least 1 hour. Yield: 14 (½-cup) servings.

Note: Substitute 1½ teaspoons vanilla extract for vanilla bean, if desired. Omit heating milk.

PER SERVING: 80 CALORIES (8% FROM FAT)
FAT 0.7G (SATURATED FAT 0.4G)
PROTEIN 3.8G   CARBOHYDRATE 14.7G
CHOLESTEROL 4MG   SODIUM 58MG

Quick Tip

In the unlikely event that you have leftover homemade sherbet or other frozen desserts, just spoon the mixture into plastic foam cups. Cover tightly and freeze. The foam insulates the contents, and the small amounts enable it to freeze quickly and solidly.

CARAMEL-PECAN ICE MILK

1½ cups sugar
¼ cup plus 2 tablespoons water
1½ tablespoons margarine
1 cup plus 2 tablespoons evaporated skimmed milk
1 teaspoon vanilla extract
⅛ teaspoon salt
2 cups 2% low-fat milk
1 cup evaporated skimmed milk
½ cup chopped pecans, toasted
1 teaspoon vanilla extract
1 (4-ounce) carton frozen egg substitute, thawed

Combine sugar and water in a medium-size heavy saucepan. Place over medium-low heat, and cook 13 minutes or until sugar dissolves. (Do not stir.) Cover, increase heat to medium, and boil 1 minute. (This will dissolve any sugar crystals clinging to sides of pan.) Uncover and boil an additional 10 minutes or until amber or golden. (Do not stir.)

Remove from heat; let stand 1 minute. Carefully add margarine, stirring until margarine melts. Gradually add 1 cup plus 2 tablespoons evaporated milk, stirring constantly. (Caramel will harden and stick to spoon.) Place pan over medium heat, and cook 3 minutes or until caramel melts and mixture is smooth, stirring constantly. Remove from heat; stir in 1 teaspoon vanilla and salt. Pour caramel sauce into a bowl; cover and chill.

Combine caramel sauce, low-fat milk, and remaining ingredients in a large bowl, and stir with a wire whisk until well blended. Pour into freezer can of a 2-quart hand-turned or electric freezer, and freeze according to manufacturer's instructions. Let ripen at least 1 hour. Yield: 13 (½-cup) servings.

PER SERVING: 188 CALORIES (25% FROM FAT)
FAT 5.2G (SATURATED FAT 1.0G)
PROTEIN 5.5G   CARBOHYDRATE 30.6G
CHOLESTEROL 5MG   SODIUM 114MG

Peach Ice Milk

PEACH ICE MILK

5 cups peeled, chopped, fresh ripe peaches
    (about 3 pounds), divided
⅔ cup sugar
1 tablespoon lemon juice
2 cups 2% low-fat milk
1 cup evaporated skimmed milk
½ cup frozen egg substitute, thawed
2 tablespoons honey
⅛ teaspoon almond extract
Fresh mint sprigs (optional)

Mash 4 cups peaches in a large bowl. Add sugar and lemon juice, stirring well; let stand 30 minutes, stirring occasionally. Add low-fat milk and next 4 ingredients, and beat at medium speed of an electric mixer until well blended; stir in remaining 1 cup peaches. Pour into freezer can of a 1-gallon hand-turned or electric freezer; freeze according to manufacturer's instructions. Let ripen at least 1 hour. Garnish with mint sprigs, if desired. Yield: 20 (½-cup) servings.

PER SERVING: 77 CALORIES (6% FROM FAT)
FAT 0.5G (SATURATED FAT 0.3G)
PROTEIN 2.7G   CARBOHYDRATE 16.3G
CHOLESTEROL 2MG   SODIUM 36MG

RASPBERRY BOMBE

1 (32-ounce) carton vanilla low-fat yogurt
1 (8-ounce) carton raspberry low-fat yogurt
Vegetable cooking spray
½ (10½-ounce) loaf commercial angel food
    cake
2 tablespoons cream sherry, divided
1 (10-ounce) package frozen raspberries in
    light syrup, thawed
¼ cup sugar
1½ teaspoons unflavored gelatin
¼ cup cold water
½ ounce semisweet chocolate, grated

Place colander in a large bowl. Line colander
with 4 layers of cheesecloth, allowing cheesecloth
to extend over edge. Combine yogurts; stir until
smooth. Pour into colander, and fold edges of
cheesecloth over to cover yogurt. Cover loosely
with plastic wrap; chill 12 hours. Remove yogurt
from colander, and discard liquid. Cover and chill.

Coat a 1½-quart bowl with cooking spray; line
with heavy-duty plastic wrap. Set aside.

Cut half of angel food cake into ½-inch-thick
slices and half into ¼-inch-thick slices. Cut all cake
slices in half diagonally to form triangles. Arrange
½-inch-thick triangles in bowl, with narrow ends
pointing to center. (Crust sides of triangles should
fit together so the center resembles a sunburst
design.) Continue lining bowl with both ½-inch
and ¼-inch triangles until inner surface of bowl is
covered. Fill any gaps with small pieces of cake.
Set remaining cake slices aside. Sprinkle 1 tablespoon sherry over cake-lined bowl. Set aside.

Press thawed raspberries through a sieve; discard
seeds. Place strained raspberries in a saucepan.
Bring to a boil; reduce heat, and simmer 20 minutes or until mixture reduces to ½ cup, stirring frequently. Add sugar, and cook, stirring constantly,
until sugar dissolves. Remove from heat.

Sprinkle gelatin over water in a small saucepan;
let stand 1 minute. Cook mixture over low heat,
stirring until gelatin dissolves, about 2 minutes.
Add raspberry mixture, stirring until well blended.

Add gelatin mixture to chilled yogurt; stir well.
Spoon yogurt mixture into cake-lined bowl. Arrange remaining cake triangles over yogurt mixture,
filling gaps with trimmed portions of cake. Sprinkle
remaining 1 tablespoon sherry over cake. Trim
cake from sides of bowl to make a smooth top.
Cover and chill at least 4 hours.

Uncover and invert bowl onto a serving platter.
Remove bowl and plastic liner. Sift grated chocolate over bombe. Yield: 10 servings.

PER SERVING: 199 CALORIES (9% FROM FAT)
FAT 2.0G (SATURATED FAT 1.2G)
PROTEIN 6.9G   CARBOHYDRATE 38.9G
CHOLESTEROL 5MG   SODIUM 149MG

FROZEN PEANUTTY DESSERT

⅔ cup chocolate wafer cookie crumbs (about
    12 cookies)
2 tablespoons sugar
1½ tablespoons reduced-calorie stick
    margarine, melted
Vegetable cooking spray
1½ quarts vanilla nonfat frozen yogurt,
    divided
⅓ cup light-colored corn syrup
⅓ cup 25% less-fat creamy peanut butter
¼ cup unsalted peanuts
1 ounce semisweet chocolate, melted

Combine first 3 ingredients in a bowl. Press
crumb mixture over bottom of an 8-inch square pan
coated with cooking spray. Soften 3 cups yogurt,
and spread over crumbs; freeze until firm.

Combine corn syrup and peanut butter in a small
bowl, stirring well. Spread over yogurt layer in pan.

Soften remaining 3 cups yogurt, and spread over
peanut butter layer. Sprinkle with peanuts, and
drizzle with chocolate. Cover and freeze until firm.
To serve, let stand at room temperature 5 minutes
before cutting. Quickly dip base of pan in warm
water to loosen crust from pan. Yield: 12 servings.

PER SERVING: 224 CALORIES (29% FROM FAT)
FAT 7.3G (SATURATED FAT 1.6G)
PROTEIN 7.5G   CARBOHYDRATE 35.6G
CHOLESTEROL 5MG   SODIUM 139MG

Frozen Peanutty Dessert

PIES & OTHER PASTRIES

*F*laky pastry filled with a chocolate cream filling and piled high with fluffy, sweet meringue—and only 268 calories a slice. No, you're not dreaming! Chocolate Meringue Pie really is low in calories, and only 27% of those come from fat.

This chapter welcomes you to low-fat versions of favorite chocolate pies as well as classics such as Lemon Meringue Pie (page 99) and Boston Cream Pie (page 100). Each has been trimmed of fat by using skim milk, egg substitute or egg whites, and reduced amounts of margarine.

We've also included fruit pies, which are rich in vitamins, minerals, and beneficial fiber. You'll find one-crust fruit pies and tarts, old-fashioned cobblers, and three fruit pastries made with naturally low-fat phyllo dough.

Chocolate Meringue Pie (recipe on page 99)

MOCHA FUDGE PIE

(pictured on cover)

⅓ cup hot water
1 tablespoon plus 1 teaspoon instant coffee
    granules, divided
½ (19.85-ounce) package light fudge brownie
    mix (about 2 cups)
2 teaspoons vanilla extract, divided
2 egg whites
Vegetable cooking spray
¾ cup 1% low-fat milk
3 tablespoons Kahlúa or other coffee-flavored
    liqueur, divided
1 (3.9-ounce) package chocolate-flavored
    instant pudding-and-pie filling mix
3 cups frozen reduced-calorie whipped
    topping, thawed and divided
Chocolate curls (optional)

Combine hot water and 2 teaspoons coffee granules in a medium bowl; stir well. Add brownie mix, 1 teaspoon vanilla, and egg whites; stir until well blended. Pour mixture into a 9-inch pieplate coated with cooking spray. Bake at 325° for 22 minutes. Let crust cool completely on a wire rack.

Combine milk, 2 tablespoons Kahlúa, 1 teaspoon coffee granules, 1 teaspoon vanilla, and pudding mix in a bowl; beat at medium speed of an electric mixer 1 minute. Fold in 1½ cups whipped topping. Spread pudding mixture over brownie crust.

Combine remaining 1 tablespoon Kahlúa and remaining 1 teaspoon coffee granules in a bowl; stir well. Gently fold in remaining 1½ cups whipped topping. Spread whipped topping mixture evenly over pudding mixture. Garnish with chocolate curls, if desired. Serve immediately, or store loosely covered in refrigerator. Yield: 8 servings.

Note: Store remaining brownie mix in a heavy-duty, zip-top plastic bag in refrigerator; reserved brownie mix can be used for another pie or to make a small pan of brownies.

PER SERVING: 292 CALORIES (22% FROM FAT)
FAT 7.0G (SATURATED FAT 5.3G)
PROTEIN 4.4G   CARBOHYDRATE 51.5G
CHOLESTEROL 1MG   SODIUM 345MG

Variation: If desired, substitute 2 tablespoons 1% low-fat milk for the Kahlúa in the pudding mixture. In the topping, omit the Kahlúa, and dissolve the coffee granules in 1 tablespoon water.

BROWNIE PIE À LA MODE

½ cup reduced-calorie stick margarine
¼ cup unsweetened cocoa
¾ cup sugar
¾ cup all-purpose flour
1 teaspoon baking powder
1½ teaspoons vanilla extract
2 egg whites
Vegetable cooking spray
1 (1-ounce) package premelted unsweetened
    chocolate
1 quart cookies-and-cream nonfat frozen
    yogurt
4 low-fat cream-filled chocolate sandwich
    cookies, cut in half (optional)

Melt margarine in a small saucepan over medium heat; stir in cocoa. Pour mixture into a large bowl. Add sugar and next 4 ingredients; stir well.

Spread batter in a 9-inch round cakepan coated with cooking spray. Bake at 350° for 20 minutes or until a wooden pick inserted in center comes out clean. Let cool in pan on a wire rack. Cut into 8 wedges.

Drizzle premelted chocolate evenly onto 8 dessert plates. Place a brownie wedge on each plate, and top each wedge with ½ cup frozen yogurt. Garnish each with a cookie half, if desired. Yield: 8 servings.

PER SERVING: 294 CALORIES (30% FROM FAT)
FAT 9.7G (SATURATED FAT 2.3G)
PROTEIN 6.7G   CARBOHYDRATE 48.6G
CHOLESTEROL 0MG   SODIUM 223MG

CHOCOLATE-CRÈME DE MENTHE PIE

3 (1-ounce) squares semisweet chocolate
2 tablespoons reduced-calorie margarine
¼ cup green crème de menthe, divided
1½ teaspoons vanilla extract, divided
1¼ cups crisp rice cereal
½ cup evaporated skimmed milk
2 tablespoons unsweetened cocoa
2 tablespoons light-colored corn syrup
1 teaspoon cornstarch
1 quart vanilla nonfat frozen yogurt, softened
Dark Chocolate Sauce
Fresh mint sprigs (optional)

Line a 9-inch pieplate with aluminum foil; fold foil under edge of pieplate. Set aside. Combine 3 squares chocolate and margarine in top of a double boiler; bring water to a boil. Reduce heat to low, and cook, stirring occasionally, until chocolate and margarine melt. Slowly add 1 tablespoon crème de menthe; cook 1 minute, stirring constantly. Remove from heat; stir in 1 teaspoon vanilla and cereal.

Spread mixture evenly over bottom and up sides of prepared pieplate. Cover and freeze 45 minutes. Peel foil from chocolate shell; return shell to pieplate. Cover and return to freezer.

Combine milk, cocoa, corn syrup, and cornstarch in a small saucepan; stir well. Bring to a boil, stirring constantly, and cook 1 minute or until mixture is thickened. Add 1 tablespoon crème de menthe, and cook an additional minute. Remove from heat; stir in remaining ½ teaspoon vanilla. Cool chocolate filling completely.

Combine frozen yogurt and remaining 2 tablespoons crème de menthe in a large bowl. Spread half of yogurt mixture in bottom of pie shell; freeze 30 minutes. Remove from freezer, and top with chocolate filling; freeze 10 minutes. Remove from freezer, and top chocolate filling with remaining yogurt mixture. Cover and freeze at least 8 hours.

Let stand at room temperature 5 minutes before serving. To serve, cut pie into wedges, and top with Dark Chocolate Sauce. Garnish with fresh mint sprigs, if desired. Yield: 8 servings.

DARK CHOCOLATE SAUCE

3 tablespoons sugar
3 tablespoons unsweetened cocoa
2 teaspoons cornstarch
1 cup water
1 teaspoon vanilla extract

Combine all ingredients in a small saucepan. Bring to a boil, stirring constantly; cook 1 minute, stirring constantly. Remove from heat, and let cool completely. Cover and let chill at least 1 hour. Yield: ¾ cup.

PER SERVING: 249 CALORIES (21% FROM FAT)
FAT 5.8G (SATURATED FAT 2.4G)
PROTEIN 6.5G   CARBOHYDRATE 45.3G
CHOLESTEROL 1MG   SODIUM 147MG

BASIC PASTRY SHELL

1¼ cups all-purpose flour
⅓ cup stick margarine
2 to 3 tablespoons cold water

Place flour in a medium bowl; cut in margarine with a pastry blender until mixture resembles coarse meal. Sprinkle cold water, 1 tablespoon at a time, evenly over surface; stir with a fork until dry ingredients are moistened. Shape dough into a ball.

Place dough between 2 sheets of heavy-duty plastic wrap, and gently press to a 4-inch circle. Chill 20 minutes. Roll dough to a 12-inch circle. Place in freezer 5 minutes or until plastic wrap can be removed easily. Remove top sheet of plastic wrap. Invert and fit pastry into a 9-inch pieplate; remove remaining sheet of plastic wrap. Fold edges of pastry under and flute; seal to edge of pieplate.

For baked pastry shell, prick bottom and sides of pastry with a fork. Bake at 450° for 10 minutes or until lightly browned. Cool on a wire rack. Yield: 1 (9-inch) pastry shell or 8 servings.

PER SERVING: 139 CALORIES (51% FROM FAT)
FAT 7.8G (SATURATED FAT 1.5G)
PROTEIN 2.1G   CARBOHYDRATE 15.0G
CHOLESTEROL 0MG   SODIUM 89MG

Lemon Meringue Pie

LEMON MERINGUE PIE

You should use only copper, metal, or glass bowls (never plastic) when beating egg whites for meringue.

⅔ cup sugar
⅓ cup cornstarch
2 cups skim milk
½ cup frozen egg substitute, thawed
2 teaspoons grated lemon rind
⅓ cup fresh lemon juice
1 baked Basic Pastry Shell (see page 97)
4 egg whites
½ teaspoon cream of tartar
½ teaspoon vanilla extract
2 tablespoons sugar
Lemon slices (optional)

Combine ⅔ cup sugar and cornstarch in a saucepan; gradually stir in milk. Cook over medium heat, stirring constantly, until mixture comes to a boil. Cook 1 minute, stirring constantly. Remove mixture from heat.

Gradually stir one-fourth of hot mixture into egg substitute; add to remaining hot mixture, stirring constantly. Cook over medium heat, stirring constantly, 2 minutes or until thickened. Remove from heat; stir in lemon rind and juice. Spoon mixture into pastry shell.

Beat egg whites, cream of tartar, and vanilla at high speed of an electric mixer until foamy. Gradually add 2 tablespoons sugar, beating until stiff peaks form. Spread meringue over hot filling, sealing to edge of crust. Bake at 325° for 25 minutes or until golden. Cool completely on a wire rack. Garnish with lemon slices, if desired. Yield: 8 servings.

PER SERVING: 276 CALORIES (26% FROM FAT)
FAT 7.9G (SATURATED FAT 1.6G)
PROTEIN 7.4G   CARBOHYDRATE 44.0G
CHOLESTEROL 1MG   SODIUM 183MG

CHOCOLATE MERINGUE PIE

(pictured on page 94)

½ cup sugar
¼ cup cornstarch
3 tablespoons unsweetened cocoa
¼ teaspoon salt
2½ cups skim milk
¼ cup frozen egg substitute, thawed
1½ teaspoons vanilla extract
1 baked Basic Pastry Shell (see page 97)
3 egg whites
¼ teaspoon cream of tartar
3 tablespoons sugar

Combine ½ cup sugar and next 3 ingredients in a saucepan; gradually stir in milk. Cook over medium heat, stirring constantly, until mixture comes to a boil. Cook 1 minute, stirring constantly. Remove from heat.

Gradually stir one-fourth of hot mixture into egg substitute; add to remaining hot mixture, stirring constantly. Cook over medium heat, stirring constantly, 2 minutes or until mixture is thickened. Remove from heat; stir in vanilla. Spoon mixture into pastry shell.

Beat egg whites and cream of tartar at high speed of an electric mixer until foamy. Gradually add 3 tablespoons sugar, 1 tablespoon at a time, beating until stiff peaks form. Spread meringue over hot filling, sealing to edge of crust. Bake at 325° for 25 minutes or until golden. Cool completely on a wire rack. Yield: 8 servings.

PER SERVING: 268 CALORIES (27% FROM FAT)
FAT 8.1G (SATURATED FAT 1.8G)
PROTEIN 7.3G   CARBOHYDRATE 41.0G
CHOLESTEROL 2MG   SODIUM 234MG

VANILLA MERINGUE PIE

Omit 3 tablespoons unsweetened cocoa, and increase vanilla extract to 1 tablespoon.

PER SERVING: 262 CALORIES (27% FROM FAT)
FAT 7.8G (SATURATED FAT 1.6G)
PROTEIN 6.7G   CARBOHYDRATE 40.3G
CHOLESTEROL 2MG   SODIUM 233MG

BUTTERSCOTCH CREAM PIE

⅔ cup all-purpose flour
⅛ teaspoon salt
⅔ cup firmly packed dark brown sugar
2 cups 1% low-fat milk
1 egg yolk
2 teaspoons margarine
1½ teaspoons vanilla extract
1 baked Basic Pastry Shell (see page 97)
½ cup frozen reduced-calorie whipped topping,
   thawed
2 teaspoons dark brown sugar

Combine flour, salt, and ⅔ cup brown sugar in a medium saucepan. Gradually add milk and egg yolk, stirring with a wire whisk until well blended. Place over medium heat, and cook, stirring constantly, 16 minutes or until thickened and bubbly. Remove from heat; stir in margarine and vanilla. Pour mixture into pastry shell; cover with plastic wrap. Chill 4 hours or until set.

Remove plastic wrap. Dollop whipped topping over filling; sprinkle dollops with 2 teaspoons brown sugar. Yield: 8 servings.

PER SERVING: 276 CALORIES (35% FROM FAT)
FAT 10.7G (SATURATED FAT 2.8G)
PROTEIN 5.7G   CARBOHYDRATE 38.8G
CHOLESTEROL 30MG   SODIUM 180MG

Health Tip

Do you have a tough time getting out the door to exercise in the morning? It helps if you can keep in mind just how good exercise is for you. Scientific research has shown that exercise helps reduce your risk of heart disease, high blood pressure, stroke, adult-onset diabetes, osteoporosis, and cancer.

BOSTON CREAM PIE

This dessert classic is not really a pie but two layers of cake filled with vanilla custard and topped with a chocolate glaze.

¼ cup stick margarine, softened
½ cup plus 3 tablespoons sugar, divided
1½ cups sifted cake flour
1½ teaspoons baking powder
¼ teaspoon salt
⅔ cup 1% low-fat milk
1 teaspoon vanilla extract
2 egg whites
Vegetable cooking spray
Vanilla Cream Filling
Chocolate Glaze

Beat margarine at medium speed of an electric mixer until creamy; gradually add ½ cup sugar, beating until light and fluffy (about 5 minutes). Combine flour, baking powder, and salt. With mixer running at low speed, add to creamed mixture alternately with milk, beginning and ending with flour mixture. Stir in vanilla.

Beat egg whites at high speed until foamy. Gradually add remaining 3 tablespoons sugar, 1 tablespoon at a time, beating until stiff peaks form. Stir one-third of egg white mixture into batter; fold in remaining egg white mixture. Pour into an 8-inch round cakepan coated with cooking spray.

Bake at 350° for 35 minutes or until a wooden pick inserted in center comes out clean. Cool in pan on a wire rack 5 minutes; remove from pan, and cool completely on a wire rack.

Split cake in half horizontally; place bottom layer, cut side up, on a serving plate. Spread with Vanilla Cream Filling; top with remaining layer. Spread Chocolate Glaze over top of cake. Chill 3 hours or until glaze is set. Yield: 10 servings.

VANILLA CREAM FILLING
½ cup sugar
1 tablespoon plus 2 teaspoons cornstarch
⅛ teaspoon salt
1¼ cups 1% low-fat milk
1 egg, lightly beaten
½ teaspoon vanilla extract

Combine first 3 ingredients in a saucepan. Add milk, stirring until well blended. Bring to a boil over medium heat; cook 1 minute, stirring constantly.

Stir one-fourth of hot milk mixture into egg; add to remaining milk mixture, stirring constantly. Cook 3 minutes or until thickened and bubbly, stirring constantly; add vanilla. Pour into a bowl; cover and chill.

CHOCOLATE GLAZE

2 tablespoons sugar
1½ tablespoons unsweetened cocoa
¾ teaspoon cornstarch
⅓ cup 1% low-fat milk
½ teaspoon vanilla extract

Combine sugar, cocoa, and cornstarch in a small saucepan. Gradually add milk, stirring with a wire whisk until well blended. Bring to a boil over medium heat, and cook 1 minute, stirring constantly; stir in vanilla.

PER SERVING: 241 CALORIES (22% FROM FAT)
FAT 5.9G (SATURATED FAT 1.7G)
PROTEIN 4.6G   CARBOHYDRATE 42.4G
CHOLESTEROL 24MG   SODIUM 232MG

Boston Cream Pie

BANANA CREAM PIE

¾ cup sifted cake flour
2 tablespoons unsweetened grated coconut,
    toasted
2 tablespoons stick margarine, melted
1 to 2 tablespoons cold water
Butter-flavored vegetable cooking spray
¾ cup plus 2 tablespoons sugar, divided
2 tablespoons cornstarch
⅛ teaspoon salt
1½ cups skim milk
1 egg
1 egg yolk
½ teaspoon vanilla extract
2 medium bananas, peeled and sliced
3 egg whites
½ teaspoon cream of tartar

Combine flour, coconut, and margarine; sprinkle water over surface of mixture, stirring with a fork until crumbly. (Do not form a ball.) Press into a 4-inch circle on heavy-duty plastic wrap. Cover with another sheet of plastic wrap. Roll into a 12-inch circle. Remove top sheet of plastic. Invert pastry into a 9-inch pieplate coated with cooking spray; remove remaining plastic. Fold edges under and flute. Prick bottom of pastry. Bake at 325° for 15 minutes; cool on a wire rack.

Combine ½ cup sugar, cornstarch, and salt in a saucepan. Add milk; stir. Cook over medium heat, stirring constantly, until thickened. Beat egg and egg yolk until thickened. Stir one-fourth of hot mixture into beaten egg; add to remaining hot mixture, stirring constantly. Cook, stirring constantly, 2 minutes or until thickened. Remove from heat; stir in vanilla. Place banana in pastry. Top with filling.

Beat egg whites and cream of tartar at high speed of an electric mixer until foamy. Add remaining ¼ cup plus 2 tablespoons sugar, 1 tablespoon at a time, beating until stiff peaks form. Spread meringue over hot filling, sealing to edge of pastry. Bake at 325° for 25 minutes. Cool completely before serving. Yield: 8 servings.

PER SERVING: 241 CALORIES (21% FROM FAT)
FAT 5.6G (SATURATED FAT 2.1G)
PROTEIN 5.4G   CARBOHYDRATE 43.4G
CHOLESTEROL 56MG   SODIUM 137MG

STREUSEL FRUIT PIE

1¼ cups plus 2 tablespoons all-purpose flour,
    divided
⅛ teaspoon salt
3 tablespoons vegetable oil
2 tablespoons ice water
2½ tablespoons lemon juice, divided
Vegetable cooking spray
¾ cup plus 2 tablespoons sugar, divided
½ teaspoon ground cinnamon
¼ teaspoon ground nutmeg, divided
3 cups peeled, chopped cooking apple
2 cups peeled, chopped pear
⅓ cup quick-cooking oats, uncooked
2 tablespoons stick margarine
½ cup (2 ounces) finely shredded reduced-fat
    sharp Cheddar cheese

Combine 1 cup flour, salt, and oil; stir until crumbly. Combine water and 1½ teaspoons lemon juice; sprinkle over flour mixture, and toss with a fork until crumbly. Press into a 4-inch circle on heavy-duty plastic wrap; cover with additional plastic wrap. Roll into an 11-inch circle.

Remove top sheet of plastic wrap. Invert dough into a 9-inch pieplate coated with cooking spray; remove remaining plastic wrap. Fold edges of pastry under and flute. Line pastry with wax paper; fill with pie weights. Bake at 400° for 8 minutes. Remove wax paper and weights; prick bottom and sides of pastry with a fork. Bake 6 minutes. Cool.

Combine 2 tablespoons flour, ½ cup sugar, cinnamon, and ⅛ teaspoon nutmeg. Toss apple and pear with remaining 2 tablespoons lemon juice; add flour mixture and stir. Spoon into pastry shell. Bake at 350° for 25 minutes.

Place oats in container of an electric blender; cover and process until ground. Combine oats, remaining ¼ cup plus 2 tablespoons sugar, ¼ cup flour, and ⅛ teaspoon nutmeg; cut in margarine with a pastry blender until mixture is crumbly. Stir in cheese. Sprinkle over fruit, and bake at 350° for 30 minutes. Let cool. Yield: 8 servings.

PER SERVING: 320 CALORIES (28% FROM FAT)
FAT 10.1G (SATURATED FAT 2.4G)
PROTEIN 5.1G   CARBOHYDRATE 54.1G
CHOLESTEROL 5MG   SODIUM 121MG

Deep-Dish Cherry Pie

DEEP-DISH CHERRY PIE

1 cup sifted cake flour
½ teaspoon baking powder
1 tablespoon sugar
¼ cup stick margarine
2 tablespoons water
Vegetable cooking spray
4 (16-ounce) cans tart cherries in water,
    undrained
⅔ cup sugar
⅓ cup cornstarch
1 teaspoon ground cinnamon
½ teaspoon almond extract

Combine first 3 ingredients in a bowl; cut in margarine with a pastry blender until mixture resembles coarse meal. Sprinkle water, 1 tablespoon at a time, over surface; stir with a fork until dry ingredients are moistened. Shape dough into a ball.

Place dough between 2 sheets of heavy-duty plastic wrap. Roll to a 12-inch circle. Remove top sheet of plastic wrap; invert pastry into a deep-dish 10-inch pieplate coated with cooking spray, and remove remaining sheet of plastic wrap. Fold edges under and flute, if desired.

Drain cherries, reserving 1¼ cups liquid. Set cherries aside. Combine reserved cherry liquid, ⅔ cup sugar, and cornstarch in a large saucepan, stirring well. Cook over medium heat, stirring constantly, until thickened and bubbly. Gently stir in cherries, cinnamon, and almond extract.

Pour cherry mixture into prepared pastry shell. Shield crust with aluminum foil, and bake at 400° for 20 minutes. Reduce heat to 375°; bake, unshielded, 25 to 30 minutes or until filling is hot and bubbly. Serve pie warm or at room temperature. Yield: 10 servings.

PER SERVING: 204 CALORIES (21% FROM FAT)
FAT 4.7G (SATURATED FAT 0.8G)
PROTEIN 1.7G   CARBOHYDRATE 37.8G
CHOLESTEROL 0MG   SODIUM 78MG

Apple Frangipane Tart

APPLE FRANGIPANE TART

½ (8-ounce) package Neufchâtel cheese, softened
¾ cup sugar, divided
½ cup ground almonds (2¼ ounces)
1 teaspoon vanilla extract
2 egg whites
5 sheets frozen phyllo pastry, thawed
Butter-flavored vegetable cooking spray
3½ medium Granny Smith apples (about 1½ pounds), each peeled, cored and halved lengthwise
2 tablespoons warm honey

Beat cheese at medium speed of an electric mixer until smooth. Add ½ cup sugar, ground almonds, vanilla, and egg whites, and beat until well blended. Set aside.

Working with 1 phyllo sheet at a time, coat each sheet with cooking spray, and fold in half crosswise, forming a 13- x 8½-inch rectangle. Gently press 1 folded sheet of phyllo into a 10-inch tart pan, allowing ends to extend over edges of pan; recoat phyllo with cooking spray. Place another folded sheet of phyllo across first sheet in a crisscross design; recoat phyllo with cooking spray. Repeat procedure with remaining 3 sheets of phyllo. Decoratively crimp edges of phyllo crust, and spread cheese mixture evenly into crust.

Cut each apple half crosswise into thin slices, leaving slices stacked together to keep shape of apple half. Place 6 apple halves around edge of tart and 1 in the center of cheese mixture; sprinkle with remaining ¼ cup sugar.

Bake at 350° for 50 minutes or until mixture is puffed and golden and apples are tender. Brush with honey before serving. Yield: 8 servings.

PER SERVING: 267 CALORIES (30% FROM FAT)
FAT 9.0G (SATURATED FAT 2.7G)
PROTEIN 5.3G   CARBOHYDRATE 44.0G
CHOLESTEROL 11MG   SODIUM 131MG

EASY FRUIT TART

1¼ cups all-purpose flour
¼ cup sugar
1 teaspoon grated lemon rind
⅓ cup stick margarine
½ cup regular oats, uncooked
1 egg, lightly beaten
2 (8-ounce) cans apricot halves in juice, undrained
1 (20-ounce) can sliced pineapple in juice, undrained
1 (16-ounce) can sliced peaches in light syrup, undrained
1 envelope unflavored gelatin
2 tablespoons sugar
2 cups fresh strawberries

Combine flour, ¼ cup sugar, and lemon rind, stirring well; cut in margarine with a pastry blender until mixture resembles coarse meal. Stir in oats. Add egg, and stir just until combined. Shape flour mixture into a ball; cover and chill at least 1 hour.

Roll dough between 2 sheets of heavy-duty plastic wrap to a 12-inch circle. Place in freezer 10 minutes or until plastic wrap can be easily removed. Remove top sheet of plastic wrap. Invert and fit pastry into a 9-inch springform pan, pressing crust about 1½ inches up sides of pan. Remove remaining plastic wrap. Prick bottom of pastry with a fork. Chill 15 minutes. Bake at 375° for 20 to 25 minutes or until lightly browned. Remove from oven, and cool completely.

Drain canned fruit, reserving ¾ cup liquid. Sprinkle gelatin over reserved liquid in a small saucepan; let stand 1 minute. Add 2 tablespoons sugar; cook over low heat, stirring constantly, until gelatin and sugar dissolve, about 2 minutes. Cool slightly.

Arrange canned fruit and strawberries in crust; pour gelatin mixture over fruit. Chill until firm. Yield: 10 servings.

PER SERVING: 254 CALORIES (26% FROM FAT)
FAT 7.2G (SATURATED FAT 1.4G)
PROTEIN 4.5G   CARBOHYDRATE 45.1G
CHOLESTEROL 22MG   SODIUM 84MG

Fresh Raspberry Tart

FRESH RASPBERRY TART

1 (8-ounce) carton red raspberry low-fat
    yogurt
1 cup sifted cake flour
1 teaspoon baking powder
2 tablespoons sugar
3 tablespoons stick margarine, cut into small
    pieces and chilled
2 to 3 tablespoons ice water
½ cup light process cream cheese, softened
½ cup sifted powdered sugar
2 tablespoons Chambord or other raspberry-
    flavored liqueur, divided
1 cup fresh raspberries
1 cup fresh blueberries
¾ cup fresh strawberries
½ cup low-sugar apple jelly
Fresh strawberry fan (optional)
Edible strawberry blossom (optional)
Fresh mint sprig (optional)

Stir yogurt, and spoon onto several layers of
heavy-duty paper towels; spread to ½-inch thickness. Cover with additional paper towels, and let
stand 15 minutes. Scrape yogurt into a bowl, using
a rubber spatula; set aside.

Combine flour, baking powder, and 2 tablespoons sugar in a bowl. Cut in margarine with a
pastry blender until mixture resembles coarse meal
and is pale yellow (about 3½ minutes). Sprinkle ice
water, 1 tablespoon at a time, over surface; toss
with a fork until dry ingredients are moistened and
mixture is crumbly. (Do not form a ball).

Gently press mixture into a 4-inch circle on
heavy-duty plastic wrap; cover with additional
heavy-duty plastic wrap, and chill 1 hour. Roll
dough, still covered, into an 11-inch circle. Place
dough in freezer 5 minutes or until plastic wrap can
easily be removed. Remove top sheet of plastic
wrap. Invert and fit dough into a 9-inch tart pan;
remove remaining sheet of plastic wrap. Prick bottom and sides of pastry with a fork. Bake at 350°
for 20 minutes or until lightly browned. Cool completely on a wire rack.

Combine drained yogurt, cream cheese, powdered sugar, and 1 tablespoon liqueur. Spoon mixture into bottom of tart shell, spreading to edges.

Arrange raspberries, blueberries, and strawberries
over yogurt mixture.

Combine jelly and remaining 1 tablespoon
liqueur in a small saucepan. Cook over medium
heat until jelly melts, stirring occasionally. Brush
jelly mixture over berries. Cover and chill at least 1
hour. If desired, garnish with a strawberry fan, a
strawberry blossom, and a fresh mint sprig. Yield:
10 servings.

PER SERVING: 191 CALORIES (28% FROM FAT)
FAT 6.0G (SATURATED FAT 2.1G)
PROTEIN 3.4G   CARBOHYDRATE 31.1G
CHOLESTEROL 7MG   SODIUM 131MG

BLACKBERRY COBBLER

5 cups fresh blackberries (about 1¾ pounds)
¾ cup sugar
2 tablespoons all-purpose flour
1 teaspoon grated lemon rind
1 tablespoon fresh lemon juice
1 teaspoon vanilla extract
Vegetable cooking spray
1 cup all-purpose flour
½ teaspoon baking powder
½ teaspoon baking soda
½ cup plain nonfat yogurt
2 tablespoons fresh lemon juice
2 tablespoons margarine, melted
1 teaspoon vanilla extract
2 egg whites

Combine first 6 ingredients in a bowl; stir gently.
Spoon blackberry mixture into an 11- x 7- x 2-inch
baking dish coated with cooking spray; set aside.

Combine 1 cup flour, baking powder, and soda in
a bowl; stir well. Combine yogurt and remaining
ingredients; add to dry ingredients, stirring just
until dry ingredients are moistened. Drop dough by
tablespoonfuls onto blackberry mixture. Bake at
400° for 30 minutes or until filling is bubbly and
crust is golden. Serve warm. Yield: 8 servings.

PER SERVING: 227 CALORIES (14% FROM FAT)
FAT 3.5G (SATURATED FAT 0.6G)
PROTEIN 4.2G   CARBOHYDRATE 45.7G
CHOLESTEROL 0MG   SODIUM 128MG

BLUEBERRY-PINEAPPLE COBBLER

2 (16-ounce) packages frozen blueberries, thawed
1 (8-ounce) can crushed pineapple in juice, undrained
½ cup sugar
2½ tablespoons cornstarch
¼ teaspoon almond extract
Butter-flavored vegetable cooking spray
½ cup all-purpose flour
½ teaspoon baking powder
⅛ teaspoon salt
¼ cup sugar
2 tablespoons reduced-calorie stick margarine
1 tablespoon skim milk
1 teaspoon all-purpose flour
1½ teaspoons sugar
¼ teaspoon ground cinnamon

Combine first 5 ingredients in a large saucepan. Bring mixture to a boil over medium heat, stirring constantly; cook 1 minute or until thickened. Remove from heat; let cool slightly. Pour blueberry mixture into a 9-inch square baking dish coated with cooking spray. Set aside.

Combine ½ cup flour and next 3 ingredients in a medium bowl; cut in margarine with a pastry blender until mixture resembles coarse meal and is pale yellow (about 3½ minutes). Add milk, stirring with a fork just until dry ingredients are moistened.

Sprinkle 1 teaspoon flour evenly over work surface. Turn dough out onto floured surface, and knead 8 to 10 times. Roll dough to ¼-inch thickness; cut into hearts with a 2-inch heart-shaped cutter or cut with a 2-inch biscuit cutter. Place hearts over blueberry mixture. Spray hearts with cooking spray.

Combine 1½ teaspoons sugar and cinnamon; sprinkle evenly over cobbler. Bake at 400° for 30 to 35 minutes or until hearts are golden and filling is bubbly. Yield: 9 servings.

PER SERVING: 184 CALORIES (12% FROM FAT)
FAT 2.4G (SATURATED FAT 0.0G)
PROTEIN 1.3G CARBOHYDRATE 41.3G
CHOLESTEROL 0MG SODIUM 60MG

OLD-FASHIONED PEACH COBBLER

¼ cup cornstarch
¼ cup unsweetened apple juice
10 cups sliced fresh peaches
1 cup unsweetened apple juice
½ cup sugar
½ teaspoon ground nutmeg
½ teaspoon almond extract
½ cup all-purpose flour
⅛ teaspoon salt
⅛ teaspoon ground nutmeg
2 tablespoons stick margarine
1 to 1½ tablespoons cold water
1 tablespoon all-purpose flour
Vegetable cooking spray
Fresh mint sprig (optional)

Combine cornstarch and ¼ cup apple juice; stir well, and set aside.

Combine peaches and next 3 ingredients in a Dutch oven. Bring to a boil; cover, reduce heat, and simmer 8 to 10 minutes or until peaches are tender. Stir in reserved cornstarch mixture. Cook, stirring constantly, until thickened and bubbly. Remove from heat, and stir in almond extract; let cool.

Combine ½ cup flour, salt, and ⅛ teaspoon nutmeg in a medium bowl; cut in margarine with a pastry blender until mixture resembles coarse meal. Sprinkle cold water, 1 tablespoon at a time, over surface; stir with a fork just until dry ingredients are moistened. Shape dough into a ball.

Sprinkle 1 tablespoon flour evenly over work surface. Roll dough to an 8-inch square on floured surface; cut into ½-inch strips.

Spoon peach mixture into an 8-inch square baking dish coated with cooking spray. Arrange pastry strips lattice-style over peach mixture. Seal pastry to edge of dish. Bake at 425° for 20 minutes or until pastry is golden and filling is bubbly. Garnish with a fresh mint sprig, if desired. Serve warm. Yield: 6 servings.

PER SERVING: 307 CALORIES (13% FROM FAT)
FAT 4.5G (SATURATED FAT 0.5G)
PROTEIN 3.2G CARBOHYDRATE 67.3G
CHOLESTEROL 0MG SODIUM 96MG

Old-Fashioned Peach Cobbler

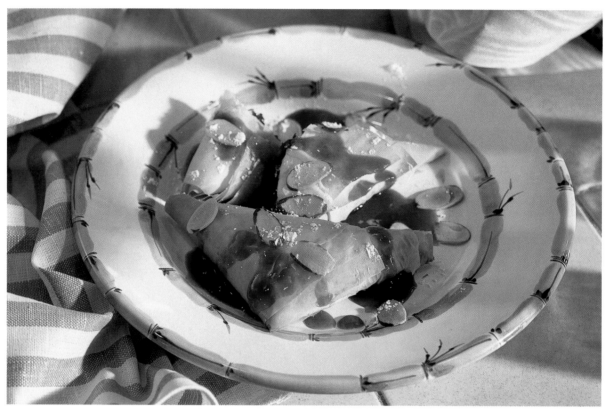

Cherry-Apple Turnovers

CHERRY-APPLE TURNOVERS

1¼ cups frozen pitted, dark, sweet cherries
1 medium Rome apple, peeled, cored, and
    coarsely chopped
¼ cup sugar
⅛ teaspoon almond extract
Dash of ground nutmeg
6 sheets frozen phyllo pastry, thawed
Butter-flavored vegetable cooking spray
½ teaspoon cornstarch
2 tablespoons sliced almonds, toasted
1 teaspoon powdered sugar

Position knife blade in food processor bowl; add cherries and apple. Pulse 4 times or until finely chopped; spoon into a bowl. Add ¼ cup sugar, almond extract, and nutmeg; stir well, and let stand 15 minutes. Press through a sieve, reserving ¼ cup plus 2 tablespoons juice. Set aside.

Working with 1 phyllo sheet at a time, cut each sheet lengthwise into 4 (3½-inch-wide) strips; lightly coat each strip with cooking spray. Stack 2 strips, one on top of the other. Spoon 1 tablespoon cherry-apple mixture onto one end of each stack; fold the left bottom corner over mixture, forming a triangle. Keep folding back and forth into a triangle to the end. Repeat with remaining cherry-apple mixture and phyllo strips. Place triangles, seam side down, on a baking sheet; coat tops with cooking spray. Bake at 400° for 15 minutes or until golden.

Combine reserved fruit juice and cornstarch in a small saucepan. Bring to a boil, and cook 1 minute, stirring constantly. Spoon over turnovers; sprinkle with almonds and powdered sugar. Serve warm or at room temperature. Yield: 6 servings.

PER SERVING: 133 CALORIES (18% FROM FAT)
FAT 2.6G (SATURATED FAT 0.3G)
PROTEIN 2.1G   CARBOHYDRATE 26.1G
CHOLESTEROL 0MG   SODIUM 93MG

MANDARIN PHYLLO BASKETS

2 sheets frozen phyllo pastry, thawed
Butter-flavored vegetable cooking spray
2 tablespoons sugar
½ cup unsweetened pineapple juice
1½ teaspoons sugar
1½ teaspoons cornstarch
1 (11-ounce) can mandarin oranges in light
    syrup, drained
1½ cups strawberry low-fat frozen yogurt

Place 1 sheet phyllo on wax paper (keep remaining phyllo covered). Lightly coat phyllo with cooking spray. Sprinkle with 1 tablespoon sugar. Layer remaining phyllo sheet on first sheet; lightly coat phyllo with cooking spray, and sprinkle with 1 tablespoon sugar.

Using a pizza cutter, cut stack of phyllo sheets crosswise into 4 (4¼-inch-wide) strips. Stack 1 strip on top of another strip to make 1 stack of 4 phyllo layers; repeat procedure with the remaining strips to make another stack of 4 phyllo layers.

Using a pizza cutter, cut 1 phyllo stack crosswise to make 3 (4½-inch) squares. Repeat procedure with remaining stack.

Place each phyllo square in a muffin cup coated with cooking spray, allowing edges to fan outward above top of cup. Bake at 325° for 8 to 10 minutes or until golden; remove from oven, and let cool.

Combine pineapple juice, 1½ teaspoons sugar, and cornstarch in a saucepan; stir. Cook mixture

over medium heat, stirring constantly, until thickened. Remove from heat, and let cool slightly. Stir in oranges.

To serve, spoon ¼ cup frozen yogurt into each phyllo basket; top yogurt with orange sauce. Serve immediately. Yield: 6 servings.

PER SERVING: 118 CALORIES (13% FROM FAT)
FAT 1.7G (SATURATED FAT 0.8G)
PROTEIN 1.8G   CARBOHYDRATE 24.3G
CHOLESTEROL 4MG   SODIUM 48MG

SPICED PEAR KISSES

1½ cups finely chopped firm ripe pear
2 teaspoons lemon juice
¼ cup firmly packed brown sugar
2 tablespoons all-purpose flour
¼ teaspoon ground cinnamon
¼ teaspoon ground nutmeg
4 sheets commercial frozen phyllo pastry,
    thawed
Vegetable cooking spray

Combine pear and lemon juice in a large bowl; toss well.

Combine brown sugar, flour, cinnamon, and nutmeg in a small bowl. Add to pear mixture, and toss to coat pear.

Working with one phyllo sheet at a time, cut each phyllo sheet in half lengthwise (keep remaining phyllo covered), and then into fourths crosswise to form 32 (6- x 4-inch) rectangles.

To assemble, lay 1 phyllo rectangle on a sheet of wax paper. Coat with cooking spray. Stack 3 more phyllo rectangles on top of first, coating each with cooking spray. Spoon one-eighth of pear mixture in center of pastry. Bring up corners of rectangle and pinch together to form a "kiss." Repeat procedure with remaining phyllo, cooking spray, and pear mixture. Place pastries on a baking sheet coated with cooking spray. Bake at 375° for 15 to 20 minutes or until golden. Serve warm. Yield: 8 servings.

PER SERVING: 72 CALORIES (10% FROM FAT)
FAT 0.8G (SATURATED FAT 0.1G)
PROTEIN 1.0G   CARBOHYDRATE 15.8G
CHOLESTEROL 0MG   SODIUM 48MG

Handle phyllo quickly and carefully, as it dries and tears easily.

PROOF OF THE PUDDING

*Y*ou loved pudding as a child, and now that it's been trimmed of excess fat and calories, you and your family can continue to indulge in this favorite dessert. The simple combination of milk, eggs, and sugar is the base for the banana, chocolate, and vanilla puddings on page 114, as well as for the dressed-up bread and rice puddings that follow. Our custards, which are similar to puddings, also retain their "comfort-food" status without the typical fat and calories.

Several recipes provide an elegant ending to a meal, such as Vanilla Floating Island (page 118)—a delicate meringue atop smooth stirred custard. Rounding out this chapter are light and airy soufflés, chiffons, and mousses, all made with few or no egg yolks and low-fat or skim milk.

Banana Pudding (recipe on page 114)

BANANA PUDDING

(pictured on page 112)

½ cup sugar
3 tablespoons cornstarch
⅛ teaspoon salt
2 cups skim milk
1 (4-ounce) carton frozen egg substitute, thawed
½ teaspoon vanilla extract
¼ teaspoon butter flavoring (optional)
28 vanilla wafers
3 medium bananas, peeled and sliced
2 egg whites
¼ teaspoon cream of tartar
3 tablespoons sugar
½ teaspoon vanilla extract

Combine first 3 ingredients in a medium-size heavy saucepan; gradually stir in milk. Cook over medium heat, stirring constantly, until mixture comes to a boil; cook 1 additional minute. Remove from heat.

Gradually stir about one-fourth of hot milk mixture into egg substitute; add to remaining hot mixture, stirring constantly. Cook over medium heat, stirring constantly, 3 minutes or until mixture thickens. Remove from heat; stir in ½ teaspoon vanilla and, if desired, butter flavoring.

Arrange half of vanilla wafers in bottom of a 1½-quart casserole; top with half of banana slices and half of custard. Repeat layering procedure with remaining vanilla wafers, banana slices, and custard.

Beat egg whites and cream of tartar at high speed of an electric mixer until foamy. Gradually add 3 tablespoons sugar, 1 tablespoon at a time, beating until stiff peaks form and sugar dissolves (2 to 4 minutes). Fold in ½ teaspoon vanilla. Spread over custard, sealing to edge of dish. Bake at 325° for 25 minutes or until golden. Yield: 8 servings.

PER SERVING: 220 CALORIES (14% FROM FAT)
FAT 3.4G (SATURATED FAT 0.7G)
PROTEIN 5.5G   CARBOHYDRATE 42.6G
CHOLESTEROL 1MG   SODIUM 160MG

CHOCOLATE PUDDING

2 (1-ounce) squares unsweetened chocolate
¾ cup sugar
¼ teaspoon salt
3½ cups skim milk, divided
¼ cup plus 1 tablespoon cornstarch
2 teaspoons vanilla extract

Melt chocolate in a heavy saucepan over low heat; stir in sugar and salt. Gradually add 3 cups milk, stirring with a wire whisk. Cook over medium heat, stirring constantly, 5 minutes.

Combine remaining ½ cup milk and cornstarch; stir well. Add to chocolate mixture. Cook over medium heat, stirring constantly, until mixture comes to a boil; boil 1 minute, stirring constantly. Remove from heat; stir in vanilla. Serve warm or chilled. Yield: 8 (½-cup) servings.

PER SERVING: 167 CALORIES (21% FROM FAT)
FAT 3.9G (SATURATED FAT 2.3G)
PROTEIN 4.4G   CARBOHYDRATE 30.8G
CHOLESTEROL 2MG   SODIUM 130MG

VANILLA PUDDING

½ cup sugar
3 tablespoons cornstarch
⅛ teaspoon salt
2¼ cups 2% low-fat milk
1 egg, lightly beaten
1 teaspoon vanilla extract

Combine first 3 ingredients in a saucepan; stir well. Combine milk and egg, stirring with a wire whisk until blended; gradually stir into sugar mixture. Bring to a boil over medium heat, stirring constantly, and cook 1 minute. Remove from heat; stir in vanilla. Serve warm. Yield: 5 (½-cup) servings.

PER SERVING: 169 CALORIES (17% FROM FAT)
FAT 3.1G (SATURATED FAT 1.6G)
PROTEIN 5.0G   CARBOHYDRATE 29.9G
CHOLESTEROL 53MG   SODIUM 127MG

BAKED LEMON PUDDING

2 egg yolks
1 cup skim milk
1½ teaspoons grated lemon rind
3 tablespoons fresh lemon juice
1½ tablespoons margarine, melted
⅔ cup sugar, divided
¼ cup plus 1 tablespoon all-purpose flour
¼ teaspoon baking powder
⅛ teaspoon salt
2 egg whites
Vegetable cooking spray
Fresh mint sprigs (optional)

Beat egg yolks at high speed of an electric mixer until thick and pale (about 2 minutes). Gradually add skim milk, lemon rind, lemon juice, and margarine; beat well.

Combine ⅓ cup sugar, flour, baking powder, and salt. Add flour mixture to egg yolk mixture; beat well.

Beat egg whites at high speed of an electric mixer until foamy. Add remaining ⅓ cup sugar, 1 tablespoon at a time, beating until stiff peaks form. Gently stir one-fourth of egg white mixture into egg yolk mixture; gently fold in remaining egg white mixture.

Pour mixture into a 1-quart casserole coated with cooking spray, and place in a large, shallow pan. Add hot water to larger pan to a depth of 1 inch. Bake at 375° for 45 minutes or until top is set. Remove dish from water, and serve warm. Garnish with mint, if desired. Yield: 4 servings.

PER SERVING: 264 CALORIES (25% FROM FAT)
FAT 7.2G (SATURATED FAT 1.7G)
PROTEIN 6.3G   CARBOHYDRATE 44.6G
CHOLESTEROL 110MG   SODIUM 205MG

Baked Lemon Pudding

Queen of Puddings

QUEEN OF PUDDINGS

5 (1-ounce) slices white bread
¼ cup plus 3 tablespoons sugar, divided
1 tablespoon reduced-calorie margarine,
   melted
1½ teaspoons grated lemon rind
3 cups skim milk
2 eggs, separated
1 teaspoon vanilla extract
Vegetable cooking spray
¼ cup plus 2 tablespoons no-sugar-added
   raspberry spread

Trim and discard crust from bread; cut bread into ¾-inch cubes, and place in a large bowl. Combine 1 tablespoon sugar, margarine, and lemon rind; drizzle over bread cubes, tossing well. Arrange bread cubes in a single layer on a baking sheet. Bake at 400° for 10 minutes or until crisp.

Combine 3 tablespoons sugar, milk, egg yolks, and vanilla in a saucepan. Place over medium heat, and cook, stirring constantly, 5 minutes or until warm. (Mixture should not thicken.)

Place ⅓ cup bread cubes into each of 6 (6-ounce) soufflé cups coated with cooking spray. Add ½ cup milk mixture to each cup. Place cups in a 13- x 9- x 2-inch pan. Pour hot water into pan to a depth of 1 inch. Bake at 350° for 1 hour or until a knife inserted in center comes out clean.

Cook raspberry spread in a small saucepan over low heat until warm. Smooth 1 tablespoon spread over top of each pudding; set aside.

Beat egg whites until foamy. Gradually add remaining 3 tablespoons sugar, 1 tablespoon at a time, beating until stiff peaks form. Spread meringue evenly over each pudding.

Bake at 350° for 10 minutes or until lightly browned. Remove cups from water. Serve warm. Yield: 6 servings.

PER SERVING: 231 CALORIES (16% FROM FAT)
FAT 4.0G (SATURATED FAT 1.0G)
PROTEIN 8.5G   CARBOHYDRATE 40.2G
CHOLESTEROL 77MG   SODIUM 240MG

APPLE-RAISIN RICE PUDDING

Short-grain rice is recommended because it has plump grains that stick together when cooked.

Vegetable cooking spray
½ cup chopped cooking apple
½ cup raisins
3 cups plus 2 teaspoons skim milk, divided
½ cup plus 1 tablespoon sugar, divided
⅓ cup short-grain rice, uncooked
1 tablespoon cornstarch
1 egg, lightly beaten
1 teaspoon vanilla extract
¼ teaspoon ground cinnamon

Coat a medium nonstick skillet with cooking spray; place over medium-high heat until hot. Add apple and raisins; sauté 1 minute. Set aside.

Combine 3 cups milk, ½ cup sugar, and rice in a large saucepan; bring to a boil. Cover, reduce heat, and simmer 15 minutes. Combine cornstarch and remaining 2 teaspoons milk, stirring well; add to rice mixture. Bring to a boil; cook 1 minute, stirring occasionally. Remove from heat.

Gradually stir about one-fourth of hot rice mixture into egg; add to remaining hot mixture, stirring constantly. Stir in apple mixture and vanilla.

Pour pudding mixture into a 1-quart baking dish coated with cooking spray. Combine remaining 1 tablespoon sugar and cinnamon; sprinkle over rice mixture. Place baking dish in a large shallow pan; add hot water to pan to a depth of 1 inch. Bake at 325° for 1 hour and 15 minutes. Remove dish from water; let cool 30 minutes before serving. Yield: 6 servings.

PER SERVING: 228 CALORIES (6% FROM FAT)
FAT 1.5G (SATURATED FAT 0.5G)
PROTEIN 6.5G   CARBOHYDRATE 48.1G
CHOLESTEROL 39MG   SODIUM 78MG

SPICY PUMPKIN CUSTARDS

⅓ cup sugar
2 tablespoons honey
1½ teaspoons ground cinnamon
1 teaspoon ground allspice
2 eggs
1 (12-ounce) can evaporated skimmed milk
1 (16-ounce) can mashed cooked pumpkin
½ cup frozen reduced-calorie whipped topping,
     thawed

Combine first 7 ingredients in a large bowl; beat at low speed of an electric mixer until smooth.

Spoon ½ cup pumpkin mixture into each of 8 (6-ounce) ramekins or custard cups. Place 4 ramekins in each of 2 (9-inch) square pans; add hot water to each pan to a depth of 1 inch. Bake at 325° for 1 hour or until set.

Remove ramekins from pans; let cool. Serve at room temperature. Top each serving with 1 tablespoon whipped topping. Yield: 8 servings.

PER SERVING: 130 CALORIES (15% FROM FAT)
FAT 2.1G (SATURATED FAT 0.9G)
PROTEIN 5.6G   CARBOHYDRATE 23.7G
CHOLESTEROL 55MG   SODIUM 71MG

Did You Know?

Even though real vanilla beans are more costly and more complicated to use than extract, they add a pure flavor to desserts that extract just can't match. That's especially important in recipes such as Vanilla Floating Island where vanilla is the predominant flavor. If you'd prefer to use extract, substitute 1½ teaspoons pure vanilla extract for each vanilla bean.

VANILLA FLOATING ISLAND

2½ cups 2% low-fat milk
1 vanilla bean, split
¼ cup sugar
1 tablespoon plus 1 teaspoon cornstarch
1 egg yolk, lightly beaten
Vegetable cooking spray
1 teaspoon sugar
4 egg whites
½ cup sugar
1 teaspoon vanilla extract
½ ounce bittersweet chocolate, grated

Pour milk into a heavy saucepan. Scrape seeds from vanilla bean; add seeds and bean to milk. Cook milk mixture over low heat 20 minutes; discard vanilla bean.

Combine ¼ cup sugar and cornstarch; add to milk mixture, stirring well. Gradually stir about one-fourth of hot milk mixture into egg yolk; add to remaining hot milk mixture, stirring constantly. Bring to a boil over medium-high heat, stirring constantly. Cook, stirring constantly, 1 minute (mixture will not be thick). Pour into a bowl; cool slightly, and cover surface with plastic wrap. Chill thoroughly (mixture will thicken slightly).

Coat a 1-quart metal bowl with cooking spray; sprinkle with 1 teaspoon sugar. Set aside.

Beat egg whites at high speed of an electric mixer until foamy. Gradually add ½ cup sugar, 1 tablespoon at a time, beating until stiff peaks form. Add vanilla extract, and beat 10 seconds. Spoon mixture into prepared bowl; gently smooth surface of mixture with a spatula. Place bowl in an 8-inch square pan; add hot water to pan to a depth of 1 inch. Bake at 325° for 20 minutes or until slightly puffed and set.

Invert island into a shallow dish. Pour sauce around island, and sprinkle with grated chocolate. Serve immediately. Yield: 5 servings.

PER SERVING: 232 CALORIES (19% FROM FAT)
FAT 5.0G (SATURATED FAT 2.7G)
PROTEIN 7.6G   CARBOHYDRATE 40.1G
CHOLESTEROL 53MG   SODIUM 105MG

CREAMY VANILLA-ALMOND CUSTARD

2½ cups skim milk
1 cup frozen egg substitute, thawed
⅓ cup sugar
1 teaspoon vanilla extract
⅛ teaspoon almond extract
Vegetable cooking spray
2 tablespoons sliced almonds, toasted

Combine first 5 ingredients in a large bowl; stir well. Pour mixture evenly into 6 (6-ounce) custard cups coated with cooking spray.

Place cups in a large shallow pan; add hot water to pan to a depth of 1 inch. Bake at 300° for 1 hour and 25 minutes or until a knife inserted in center comes out clean. Remove cups from water; cool slightly. Cover and chill thoroughly.

Sprinkle evenly with almonds just before serving. Yield: 6 servings.

PER SERVING: 128 CALORIES (18% FROM FAT)
FAT 2.6G (SATURATED FAT 0.4G)
PROTEIN 8.3G   CARBOHYDRATE 17.8G
CHOLESTEROL 2MG   SODIUM 114MG

Creamy Vanilla-Almond Custard

Ginger Crème Caramel

GINGER CRÈME CARAMEL

¾ cup sugar
¼ cup water
¼ teaspoon cream of tartar
2½ cups 1% low-fat milk
1¼ cups frozen egg substitute, thawed
½ cup sugar
2 tablespoons minced crystallized ginger

Combine first 3 ingredients in a small saucepan; stir well. Cook over medium-low heat, stirring constantly, until sugar dissolves. Bring to a boil; cook, without stirring, until mixture is caramel-colored and candy thermometer registers 340°. Remove from heat, and immediately pour mixture into an 8-inch round cakepan, tilting to coat bottom of pan evenly; set aside.

Place low-fat milk in a heavy saucepan; cook over medium heat until thoroughly heated. Combine egg substitute and ½ cup sugar in a medium bowl; stir with a wire whisk until well blended. Gradually add warm milk, stirring well. Stir in ginger. Pour into prepared pan.

Place pan in a 13- x 9- x 2-inch pan; pour hot water into pan to a depth of 1 inch. Place in a 350° oven. Reduce heat to 325°, and bake 1 hour or until knife inserted halfway between center and edge comes out clean. Remove pan from water, and let cool on a wire rack.

Cover and chill 8 hours. To serve, unmold custard and sauce onto a serving platter. Yield: 8 servings.

PER SERVING: 175 CALORIES (4% FROM FAT)
FAT 0.8G (SATURATED FAT 0.5G)
PROTEIN 6.2G   CARBOHYDRATE 36.4G
CHOLESTEROL 3MG   SODIUM 102MG

RASPBERRY CUSTARD BRÛLÉE

2 cups fresh raspberries
3 tablespoons sugar
1 tablespoon cornstarch
1½ cups skim milk
1 egg, lightly beaten
3 tablespoons nonfat sour cream
¾ teaspoon vanilla extract
2 tablespoons brown sugar

Divide raspberries evenly among 6 (4-ounce) ovenproof ramekins or custard cups. Set aside.

Combine sugar and cornstarch in a small saucepan; stir well. Combine milk and egg in a small bowl, stirring well; add to sugar mixture. Cook over medium heat, stirring constantly, until mixture comes to a boil. Remove from heat; let cool 5 minutes. Stir in sour cream and vanilla.

Spoon custard mixture evenly over raspberries. Place ramekins on a baking sheet. Sprinkle each with 1 teaspoon brown sugar. Broil 5½ inches from heat 2 minutes or until sugar melts. Serve immediately. Yield: 6 servings.

PER SERVING: 101 CALORIES (11% FROM FAT)
FAT 1.2G (SATURATED FAT 0.3G)
PROTEIN 4.0G   CARBOHYDRATE 18.8G
CHOLESTEROL 38MG   SODIUM 49MG

FYI

Custards require slow cooking and gentle heat to prevent the mixture from curdling or separating. Baking custards in a hot water bath helps protect the creamy, smooth texture. Stovetop custards require frequent, often constant, stirring.

ORANGE FLAN

¾ cup sugar, divided
½ teaspoon grated orange rind
1 (12-ounce) can evaporated skimmed milk
⅔ cup 1% low-fat milk
¼ cup unsweetened orange juice
1 tablespoon Triple Sec or other orange-flavored liqueur
1 cup frozen egg substitute, thawed
1 teaspoon vanilla extract
⅛ teaspoon salt

Place ½ cup sugar in a medium saucepan. Cook over medium heat, stirring constantly, until sugar melts and is light brown. Pour melted sugar evenly into 8 (6-ounce) custard cups, tilting to coat bottoms of cups. Sprinkle grated orange rind evenly over bottoms of cups.

Combine evaporated milk, low-fat milk, orange juice, and Triple Sec in a medium saucepan. Cook over medium heat, stirring constantly, until mixture is thoroughly heated.

Combine remaining ¼ cup sugar, egg substitute, vanilla, and salt in a medium bowl. Beat at medium speed of an electric mixer until blended. Gradually stir 1 cup hot milk mixture into egg substitute mixture; add to remaining hot mixture, stirring constantly. Pour evenly into prepared custard cups.

Place custard cups in 2 (9-inch) square pans; pour hot water into pans to a depth of 1 inch. Bake at 350° for 55 minutes or until a knife inserted in center comes out clean. Remove cups from water, and let cool on wire racks.

Cover and chill at least 4 hours. To serve, loosen edges of custards with a knife; invert onto individual serving plates. Yield: 8 servings.

PER SERVING: 139 CALORIES (4% FROM FAT)
FAT 0.6G (SATURATED FAT 0.4G)
PROTEIN 7.0G   CARBOHYDRATE 26.5G
CHOLESTEROL 3MG   SODIUM 143MG

Coat each soufflé dish with cooking spray, and sprinkle with sugar.

Beat egg whites and sugar until stiff peaks form.

Gently fold egg white mixture into cooled custard.

After freezing for 2 hours, wrap the soufflés in aluminum foil.

Banana-Walnut Soufflé

BANANA-WALNUT SOUFFLÉ

Vegetable cooking spray
2 teaspoons sugar
2 tablespoons reduced-calorie margarine
¼ cup all-purpose flour
¾ cup 1% low-fat milk
¼ cup plus 2 tablespoons sugar, divided
¾ cup mashed ripe banana (about 2 medium)
¼ cup chopped walnuts, toasted
1 teaspoon vanilla extract
½ teaspoon lemon juice
6 egg whites
⅛ teaspoon cream of tartar

Coat 8 (6-ounce) soufflé dishes or custard cups with cooking spray; sprinkle each with ¼ teaspoon sugar. Set aside.

Melt margarine in a saucepan over medium heat; add flour. Cook 1 minute, stirring constantly with a wire whisk. Gradually add milk and 3 tablespoons sugar, stirring constantly. Cook, stirring constantly, until mixture is thickened and bubbly. Remove from heat; pour into a large bowl.

Combine banana and next 3 ingredients in a bowl, stirring well. Add to milk mixture; stir well. Cover with plastic wrap, and let cool completely.

Beat egg whites and cream of tartar at high speed of an electric mixer until soft peaks form. Gradually add remaining 3 tablespoons sugar, 1 tablespoon at a time, beating until stiff peaks form.

Gently fold egg white mixture into banana mixture. Spoon evenly into prepared soufflé dishes. Freeze until firm (about 2 hours); wrap with heavy-duty aluminum foil. Freeze up to 2 weeks.

Place frozen soufflés in 2 (9-inch) square pans. Add hot water to pans to depth of 1 inch. Bake at 350° for 40 minutes or until puffed and set. Serve immediately. Yield: 8 servings.

PER SERVING: 136 CALORIES (30% FROM FAT)
FAT 4.5G (SATURATED FAT 0.6G)
PROTEIN 4.8G   CARBOHYDRATE 20.2G
CHOLESTEROL 1MG   SODIUM 79MG

WARM CHOCOLATE SOUFFLÉS

Vegetable cooking spray
⅓ cup plus 1 tablespoon sugar
3 tablespoons unsweetened cocoa
2 tablespoons all-purpose flour
¾ cup evaporated skimmed milk
2 egg yolks
4 egg whites
½ teaspoon cream of tartar
Custard Sauce (see page 136)

Cut 6 pieces of aluminum foil long enough to fit around 6 (6-ounce) ramekins or custard cups, allowing a 1-inch overlap; fold foil lengthwise into fifths. Lightly coat one side of foil and bottom of ramekins with cooking spray. Wrap a foil strip around outside of each ramekin, coated side against ramekin, allowing it to extend 1 inch above rim to form a collar; secure with string.

Combine sugar, cocoa, and flour in a saucepan. Gradually add milk, stirring with a wire whisk until blended. Cook over medium heat, stirring constantly, until mixture is thickened and bubbly.

Beat 2 egg yolks until thick and pale. Gradually stir one-fourth of hot mixture into egg yolks; add to remaining hot mixture, stirring constantly. Remove from heat.

Beat egg whites and cream of tartar in a large bowl at high speed of an electric mixer until stiff peaks form. Gently fold one-fourth of egg white mixture into chocolate mixture. Gently fold remaining egg white mixture into chocolate mixture. Spoon evenly into prepared ramekins. Bake at 375° for 18 minutes or until puffed. Top soufflés evenly with Custard Sauce. Serve immediately. Yield: 6 servings.

PER SERVING: 179 CALORIES (16% FROM FAT)
FAT 3.2G (SATURATED FAT 1.1G)
PROTEIN 8.2G   CARBOHYDRATE 29.0G
CHOLESTEROL 111MG   SODIUM 93MG

ORANGE CHIFFON

⅔ cup evaporated skimmed milk
1 envelope unflavored gelatin
1 cup fresh orange juice
1 teaspoon grated orange rind
3 tablespoons powdered sugar

Chill milk 8 hours. Sprinkle gelatin over juice in a nonaluminum saucepan; let stand 1 minute. Cook over medium heat, stirring until gelatin dissolves, about 2 minutes. Remove from heat, and stir in orange rind. Let cool completely.

Place milk in a large chilled bowl; beat at high speed of an electric mixer until soft peaks form. Gradually add powdered sugar, 1 tablespoon at a time, beating until stiff peaks form. Gently fold in orange juice mixture. Spoon into individual serving dishes; chill until set. Yield: 9 (½-cup) servings.

PER SERVING: 40 CALORIES (2% FROM FAT)
FAT 0.1G (SATURATED FAT 0.0G)
PROTEIN 2.3G   CARBOHYDRATE 7.7G
CHOLESTEROL 1MG   SODIUM 23MG

VANILLA MOUSSE WITH BLUEBERRY SAUCE

2½ cups fresh blueberries
¼ cup sugar
¼ cup water
1 teaspoon cornstarch
1 envelope unflavored gelatin
¾ cup plus 2 tablespoons skim milk
1 (8-ounce) carton vanilla low-fat yogurt
½ (8-ounce) package Neufchâtel cheese, softened
2½ tablespoons sugar
Vegetable cooking spray

Combine blueberries, ¼ cup sugar, water, and cornstarch in a saucepan. Cook over medium heat, stirring constantly, 5 minutes or until sugar dissolves and mixture is thickened. Remove from heat, and let cool slightly. Cover blueberry mixture, and chill thoroughly.

Sprinkle gelatin over milk in a small saucepan; let stand 1 minute. Cook mixture over low heat, stirring until gelatin dissolves, about 2 minutes. Remove pan from heat; set aside, and let cool.

Position knife blade in food processor bowl. Add yogurt, cheese, and 2½ tablespoons sugar; process 1 minute. Add gelatin mixture to yogurt mixture, and process 1 minute or until mixture is smooth. Spoon yogurt mixture into a 3-cup mold coated with cooking spray. Cover and chill until firm.

Unmold mousse onto a serving plate. Serve with blueberry sauce. Yield: 6 servings.

PER SERVING: 189 CALORIES (25% FROM FAT)
FAT 5.3G (SATURATED FAT 3.2G)
PROTEIN 6.4G   CARBOHYDRATE 30.6G
CHOLESTEROL 17MG   SODIUM 124MG

STRAWBERRY MOUSSE

1 envelope unflavored gelatin
½ cup skim milk
¼ cup sugar
4 cups fresh strawberries, divided
⅓ cup nonfat sour cream
¼ cup plus 1 tablespoon frozen reduced-calorie whipped topping, thawed

Sprinkle gelatin over milk in a small saucepan; let stand 1 minute. Cook over low heat, stirring until gelatin dissolves, about 2 minutes. Remove from heat; add sugar, stirring until sugar dissolves.

Reserve 5 strawberries for garnish; set aside. Place remaining strawberries in container of an electric blender or food processor; cover and process until smooth. Add gelatin mixture and sour cream; cover and process until blended.

Spoon strawberry mixture evenly into 5 (4-ounce) parfait glasses. Cover and chill until set. Top each parfait with 1 tablespoon whipped topping and a reserved strawberry. Yield: 5 (½-cup) servings.

PER SERVING: 100 CALORIES (8% FROM FAT)
FAT 0.9G (SATURATED FAT 0.4G)
PROTEIN 3.8G   CARBOHYDRATE 19.8G
CHOLESTEROL 1MG   SODIUM 29MG

Strawberry Mousse

SWEET POTPOURRI

*L*ast but not least, this medley of sweets includes cold beverages, fruit soups, and an assortment of delicious sauces. Your children will love Banana Split Smoothie or Berry Refresher (page 128) at snack-time as well as for dessert. These beverages are loaded with nutrients from pureed fruit and fruit juice.

Fresh fruit also stars in colorful soups like Citrus Cantaloupe Soup (page 133). With little effort, you'll have a unique dessert that looks and tastes impressive.

Sauces such as Raspberry Peach Sauce (page 134) and luscious Caramel Sauce (page 136) can turn a simple angel food or pound cake into a gourmet indulgence. And don't overlook Mississippi Mud Sauce (page 140) for a lightened version of a favorite chocolate sauce.

Berry Peach Soup (recipe on page 133)

BERRY REFRESHER

1 cup halved fresh or thawed frozen
   strawberries
½ cup unsweetened orange juice
2 tablespoons powdered sugar
1 (8-ounce) carton raspberry low-fat yogurt
10 ice cubes

Combine all ingredients in container of an electric blender; cover and process until smooth. Serve immediately. Yield: 3 (1-cup) servings.

PER SERVING: 128 CALORIES (8% FROM FAT)
FAT 1.1G (SATURATED FAT 0.6G)
PROTEIN 3.6G   CARBOHYDRATE 27.0G
CHOLESTEROL 3MG   SODIUM 41MG

TROPICAL MANGO COOLER

1 cup cubed ripe mango
1 cup apricot nectar
¼ cup frozen tangerine juice concentrate,
   thawed and undiluted
1 tablespoon fresh lime juice
2 teaspoons sugar
¼ teaspoon almond extract
¼ teaspoon vanilla extract
¼ teaspoon rum flavoring
2 cups club soda, chilled

Combine first 8 ingredients in container of an electric blender; cover and process until smooth. Transfer mixture to a pitcher.

Stir in club soda just before serving. Serve over ice. Yield: 4 (1-cup) servings.

PER SERVING: 106 CALORIES (2% FROM FAT)
FAT 0.2G (SATURATED FAT 0.0G)
PROTEIN 0.7G   CARBOHYDRATE 26.3G
CHOLESTEROL 0MG   SODIUM 27MG

SPARKLING RASPBERRY SPRITZER

1 (16-ounce) package frozen unsweetened
   raspberries, thawed
1 (24-ounce) bottle white grape juice, chilled
1¾ cups club soda, chilled

Place raspberries in container of an electric blender; cover and process until smooth. Pour raspberries through a wire-mesh strainer into a bowl, discarding seeds.

Combine raspberry puree and grape juice in a medium pitcher, stirring well. Stir in club soda just before serving. Serve immediately. Yield: 6 (1-cup) servings.

PER SERVING: 112 CALORIES (3% FROM FAT)
FAT 0.4G (SATURATED FAT 0.0G)
PROTEIN 0.7G   CARBOHYDRATE 28.0G
CHOLESTEROL 0MG   SODIUM 18MG

BANANA SPLIT SMOOTHIE

1¼ cups peeled, sliced ripe banana (about 2
   medium)
1 (8-ounce) can crushed pineapple in juice,
   undrained
1 cup crushed ice
½ cup unsweetened orange juice
1 teaspoon sugar
1 (8-ounce) carton vanilla low-fat yogurt

Combine first 5 ingredients in container of an electric blender. Cover and process until smooth. Add yogurt; process until blended. Serve immediately. Yield: 4 (1-cup) servings.

PER SERVING: 138 CALORIES (7% FROM FAT)
FAT 1.0G (SATURATED FAT 0.5G)
PROTEIN 3.7G   CARBOHYDRATE 30.7G
CHOLESTEROL 3MG   SODIUM 39MG

Clockwise from left: *Banana Split Smoothie, Tropical Mango Cooler, and Sparkling Raspberry Spritzer*

From left: *Tropical Milkshake, Strawberry Milkshake, and Creamy Vanilla Milkshake*

CREAMY VANILLA MILKSHAKE

4 cups vanilla nonfat frozen yogurt
1¾ cups skim milk
½ teaspoon vanilla extract

Combine all ingredients in container of an electric blender; cover and process until smooth. Serve immediately. Yield: 5 (1-cup) servings.

PER SERVING: 162 CALORIES (1% FROM FAT)
FAT 0.1G (SATURATED FAT 0.1G)
PROTEIN 8.4G   CARBOHYDRATE 33.2G
CHOLESTEROL 2MG   SODIUM 141MG

CHOCOLATE MILKSHAKE
Substitute 4½ cups chocolate nonfat frozen yogurt for vanilla frozen yogurt; add ⅓ cup chocolate syrup. Omit vanilla. Yield: 6 (1-cup) servings.

PER SERVING: 196 CALORIES (1% FROM FAT)
FAT 0.3G (SATURATED FAT 0.1G)
PROTEIN 8.4G   CARBOHYDRATE 41.6G
CHOLESTEROL 1MG   SODIUM 142MG

STRAWBERRY MILKSHAKE
Substitute strawberry nonfat frozen yogurt for vanilla frozen yogurt. Omit vanilla. Add 1½ cups fresh strawberries to blender. Process until smooth. Yield: 6 (1-cup) servings.

PER SERVING: 145 CALORIES (2% FROM FAT)
FAT 0.3G (SATURATED FAT 0.1G)
PROTEIN 7.2G   CARBOHYDRATE 30.1G
CHOLESTEROL 1MG   SODIUM 118MG

TROPICAL MILKSHAKE
Omit vanilla extract. Add 1 (8-ounce) can unsweetened crushed pineapple, undrained; 1 cup cubed papaya; ½ cup unsweetened pineapple juice; and ½ teaspoon rum extract to ingredients in blender. Yield: 8 (1-cup) servings.

PER SERVING: 135 CALORIES (1% FROM FAT)
FAT 0.2G (SATURATED FAT 0.1G)
PROTEIN 5.6G   CARBOHYDRATE 29.1G
CHOLESTEROL 1MG   SODIUM 89MG

MARSHMALLOW CREAM NOG

4 cups skim milk
½ cup marshmallow cream
3 tablespoons sugar
1 (4-inch) piece vanilla bean, split lengthwise
1⅔ cups frozen egg substitute, thawed
½ cup bourbon
½ teaspoon freshly grated nutmeg
2 cups low-fat vanilla ice cream, softened

Combine first 4 ingredients in a large saucepan; stir well. Cook over medium-low heat until marshmallow cream melts. Gradually stir about one-fourth of hot mixture into egg substitute; add to remaining hot mixture, stirring constantly. Cook mixture over low heat, stirring constantly, 1 to 2 minutes or until mixture thickens.
Remove mixture from heat; stir in bourbon and nutmeg. Let cool. Cover and chill 3 hours. Remove and discard vanilla bean; stir in ice cream just before serving. Yield: 16 (½-cup) servings.

PER SERVING: 113 CALORIES (7% FROM FAT)
FAT 0.9G (SATURATED FAT 0.5G)
PROTEIN 5.3G   CARBOHYDRATE 12.6G
CHOLESTEROL 4MG   SODIUM 84MG

ICED VANILLA COFFEE

8 cups hot brewed hazelnut-flavored coffee
½ cup sugar
1 tablespoon vanilla extract
2 cups skim milk
⅔ cup vanilla low-fat frozen yogurt, softened

Combine coffee, sugar, and vanilla, stirring until sugar dissolves. Stir in milk; cover and chill. To serve, pour 1 cup coffee into a glass, and top with 1 tablespoon frozen yogurt. Yield: 10 (1-cup) servings.

PER SERVING: 70 CALORIES (3% FROM FAT)
FAT 0.2G (SATURATED FAT 0.2G)
PROTEIN 2.0G   CARBOHYDRATE 14.7G
CHOLESTEROL 2MG   SODIUM 32MG

Fresh Blueberry Soup

FRESH BLUEBERRY SOUP

2 cups fresh blueberries
2½ cups unsweetened grape juice
¼ cup sugar
1 (3-inch) stick cinnamon
1 tablespoon plus 2 teaspoons cornstarch
2 tablespoons water
¼ teaspoon ground cardamom
3 tablespoons crème de cassis
1 tablespoon plus 1 teaspoon vanilla low-fat
     yogurt

Combine first 4 ingredients in a medium saucepan. Bring mixture to a boil; cover, reduce heat, and simmer 5 minutes.

Combine cornstarch and water; stir well. Add cornstarch mixture and cardamom to blueberry mixture, stirring well. Cook, stirring constantly, until mixture is thickened and bubbly. Remove from heat, and let cool.

Stir in crème de cassis. Cover and chill thoroughly. Remove and discard cinnamon stick before serving. Ladle soup into individual bowls; drizzle 1 teaspoon yogurt in 3 small circles over each serving. Pull a wooden pick through each circle, forming hearts. Yield: 4 (1-cup) servings.

PER SERVING: 226 CALORIES (1% FROM FAT)
FAT 0.3G (SATURATED FAT 0.0G)
PROTEIN 0.6G   CARBOHYDRATE 54.6G
CHOLESTEROL 0MG   SODIUM 13MG

BERRY PEACH SOUP

(pictured on page 126)

1 cup fresh raspberries
3 cups fresh or frozen sliced peaches, thawed
3 tablespoons lemon juice
1 cup peach nectar
1 (8-ounce) carton plain nonfat yogurt
1 teaspoon almond extract

Place raspberries in container of an electric blender or food processor. Cover and process until smooth. Press berry mixture through a wire mesh strainer, discarding seeds. Cover and chill.

Place peaches and lemon juice in container of an electric blender; cover and process until smooth. Pour into a large bowl. Stir in nectar, yogurt, and almond extract. Cover and chill.

Spoon peach mixture into individual soup bowls. Drizzle 1 tablespoon raspberry sauce in a spiral on top of each serving. Draw a wooden pick through sauce, spoke-fashion, at regular intervals to create a webbed effect. Yield: 4 (1-cup) servings.

PER SERVING: 141 CALORIES (3% FROM FAT)
FAT 0.5G (SATURATED FAT 0.1G)
PROTEIN 4.6G   CARBOHYDRATE 31.7G
CHOLESTEROL 1MG   SODIUM 48MG

CITRUS CANTALOUPE SOUP

This soup is refreshing and light. Serve it as an appetizer or dessert.

3 cups cubed cantaloupe (about 1 small)
1 cup unsweetened orange juice
¼ cup vanilla low-fat yogurt
2 teaspoons honey
¼ teaspoon ground ginger
⅛ teaspoon freshly grated nutmeg
1 tablespoon plus 1 teaspoon vanilla low-fat
     yogurt
Fresh mint leaves (optional)
Edible flowers (optional)

Place first 6 ingredients in container of an electric blender or food processor; cover and process until smooth. Transfer to a bowl. Cover and chill.

To serve, ladle soup into individual bowls. Top each serving with 1 teaspoon yogurt. If desired, garnish with mint leaves and edible flowers. Yield: 4 (1-cup) servings.

PER SERVING: 103 CALORIES (6% FROM FAT)
FAT 0.7G (SATURATED FAT 0.4G)
PROTEIN 2.6G   CARBOHYDRATE 23.6G
CHOLESTEROL 1MG   SODIUM 25MG

FRESH BLUEBERRY SAUCE

1¾ cups unsweetened grape juice, divided
2 cups fresh blueberries, divided
1 tablespoon frozen orange juice concentrate, undiluted
⅛ teaspoon ground ginger
⅛ teaspoon ground cinnamon
2 tablespoons cornstarch

Combine 1 cup grape juice, 1 cup blueberries, and next 3 ingredients in a medium saucepan. Bring mixture to a boil; reduce heat, and simmer 3 to 5 minutes or until blueberry skins pop, stirring occasionally.

Combine cornstarch and remaining ¾ cup grape juice, stirring until smooth; add to blueberry mixture. Cook over medium heat, stirring constantly, until thickened. Remove from heat; let cool completely. Stir in remaining 1 cup blueberries. Serve chilled over nonfat ice cream, nonfat frozen yogurt, or angel food cake. Yield: 2¾ cups.

PER TABLESPOON: 13 CALORIES (0% FROM FAT)
FAT 0.0G (SATURATED FAT 0.0G)
PROTEIN 0.1G   CARBOHYDRATE 3.3G
CHOLESTEROL 0MG   SODIUM 1MG

RASPBERRY PEACH SAUCE

1 cup peeled, sliced fresh peaches
¾ cup peach nectar
¼ cup water
1 tablespoon cornstarch
⅛ teaspoon almond extract
½ cup fresh raspberries

Combine peaches and peach nectar in a medium saucepan. Bring to a boil; reduce heat to medium, and cook 5 minutes or until peaches are tender, stirring occasionally.

Combine water and cornstarch in a small bowl, stirring until smooth. Add cornstarch mixture to peach mixture. Cook, stirring constantly, until thickened and bubbly. Remove from heat; stir in almond extract. Let cool completely.

Stir in raspberries. Serve chilled over nonfat ice cream, nonfat frozen yogurt, angel food cake, or fat-free pound cake. Yield: 2 cups.

PER TABLESPOON: 8 CALORIES (0% FROM FAT)
FAT 0.0G (SATURATED FAT 0.0G)
PROTEIN 0.1G   CARBOHYDRATE 1.9G
CHOLESTEROL 0MG   SODIUM 0MG

FRESH STRAWBERRY SAUCE

4 cups fresh strawberries, sliced
¼ cup sugar
1 tablespoon cornstarch
½ teaspoon almond extract
Frozen reduced-calorie whipped topping, thawed (optional)

Combine fresh strawberries and sugar in a small bowl. Let stand until syrup forms (about 1 hour). Drain syrup into a 2-cup glass measure, reserving strawberries. Add water to strawberry syrup to make 1½ cups.

Combine syrup mixture and cornstarch in a small saucepan; stir well. Cook over medium heat, stirring constantly, until smooth and thickened. Cover and chill.

Stir in reserved strawberries and almond extract before serving. Serve strawberry sauce over fat-free pound cake, commercial shortcakes, or nonfat ice cream. Garnish with whipped topping, if desired. Yield: 3 cups.

PER TABLESPOON: 8 CALORIES (0% FROM FAT)
FAT 0.0G (SATURATED FAT 0.0G)
PROTEIN 0.1G   CARBOHYDRATE 2.1G
CHOLESTEROL 0MG   SODIUM 0MG

Fresh Strawberry Sauce

CUSTARD SAUCE

*Try spooning this easy stirred custard over warm
Chocolate Soufflés (page 123) and serving
immediately.*

3 tablespoons sugar
1 teaspoon cornstarch
¾ cup skim milk
1 egg yolk, lightly beaten
1 teaspoon vanilla extract

Combine sugar and cornstarch in a small saucepan; gradually stir in milk. Cook over medium heat,
stirring constantly, until mixture is thickened.
Gradually stir one-fourth of hot mixture into beaten
egg yolk; add to remaining hot mixture. Reduce
heat to low, and cook 1 minute, stirring constantly.
Remove from heat; stir in vanilla. Serve warm over
soufflés, angel food cake, or fresh fruit. Yield: 1 cup.

PER TABLESPOON: 18 CALORIES (15% FROM FAT)
FAT 0.3G (SATURATED FAT 0.1G)
PROTEIN 0.6G   CARBOHYDRATE 3.1G
CHOLESTEROL 14MG   SODIUM 6MG

LEMON DESSERT SAUCE

½ cup sugar
2 tablespoons cornstarch
1 cup water
2 teaspoons grated lemon rind
⅓ cup fresh lemon juice

Combine sugar and cornstarch in a saucepan.
Gradually stir in water. Cook over medium heat,
stirring constantly, until mixture comes to a boil.
Reduce heat, and simmer 1 minute, stirring constantly. Remove from heat; stir in lemon rind and
lemon juice. Serve warm or chilled over angel food
cake or fresh fruit. Yield: 1½ cups.

PER TABLESPOON: 19 CALORIES (0% FROM FAT)
FAT 0.0G (SATURATED FAT 0.0G)
PROTEIN 0.0G   CARBOHYDRATE 5.1G
CHOLESTEROL 0MG   SODIUM 0MG

CARAMEL SAUCE

1 cup sugar
¼ cup water
1 tablespoon margarine
¾ cup evaporated skimmed milk
½ teaspoon vanilla extract
Dash of salt

Combine sugar and water in a medium-size
heavy saucepan. Place over medium-low heat, and
cook 13 minutes or until sugar dissolves. (Do not
stir.) Cover, increase heat to medium, and boil 1
minute. (This will dissolve any sugar crystals clinging to sides of pan.) Uncover and boil an additional
10 minutes or until amber or golden. (Do not stir.)
Remove from heat; let stand 1 minute. Carefully
add margarine, stirring until margarine melts.
Gradually add milk, stirring constantly. (Caramel
will harden and stick to spoon.)
Place pan over medium heat; cook, stirring constantly, 3 minutes or until caramel melts and is
smooth. Remove from heat; stir in vanilla and salt.
Pour into a bowl; cover and chill. Serve over nonfat
ice cream or fat-free pound cake. Yield: 1¼ cups.

PER TABLESPOON: 52 CALORIES (10% FROM FAT)
FAT 0.6G (SATURATED FAT 0.1G)
PROTEIN 0.7G   CARBOHYDRATE 11.1G
CHOLESTEROL 0MG   SODIUM 32MG

Calorie Countdown

It's easier said than done, but the truth is to
lose weight you must burn more calories than
you take in. One of the best ways to do this is
to combine low-fat foods and exercise. Plan
on losing no more than 2 pounds a week in
order to safely reach your weight-loss goal.
This will also make it easier for you to maintain your desired weight.

Cook over medium-low heat until sugar completely dissolves.

Boil, covered, over medium heat to dissolve sugar on sides.

Boil an additional 8 to 10 minutes or until golden.

Watch the syrup closely—it can darken quickly.

Don't panic when the caramel clumps on the spoon.

Cook, stirring constantly, over medium heat until smooth.

Caramel Sauce

PRALINE-PECAN SAUCE

½ cup firmly packed dark brown sugar
1 tablespoon cornstarch
1 cup evaporated skimmed milk
¼ cup chopped pecans, toasted
1 tablespoon reduced-calorie margarine
2 teaspoons vanilla extract

Combine brown sugar and cornstarch in a medium saucepan. Gradually stir in evaporated milk. Cook over medium heat, stirring constantly, until mixture comes to a boil and thickens slightly. Remove from heat.

Add pecans, margarine, and vanilla, stirring until margarine melts. Serve warm over nonfat ice cream, angel food cake, or fat-free pound cake. Yield: 1½ cups plus 2 tablespoons.

PER TABLESPOON: 36 CALORIES (25% FROM FAT)
FAT 1.0G (SATURATED FAT 0.1G)
PROTEIN 0.8G   CARBOHYDRATE 5.8G
CHOLESTEROL 0MG   SODIUM 17MG

KAHLÚA-PECAN SAUCE

¼ cup sugar
1 tablespoon cornstarch
⅔ cup water
¼ cup Kahlúa or other coffee-flavored liqueur
¼ cup chopped pecans, toasted

Combine sugar and cornstarch in a small saucepan. Gradually stir in water. Cook over medium heat, stirring constantly, until mixture comes to a boil. Reduce heat, and simmer, stirring constantly, 2 minutes or until mixture is thickened.

Remove pan from heat; stir in Kahlúa and pecans. Serve warm or chilled over nonfat ice cream, nonfat frozen yogurt, angel food cake, or fat-free pound cake. Yield: 1 cup plus 2 tablespoons.

PER TABLESPOON: 30 CALORIES (27% FROM FAT)
FAT 0.9G (SATURATED FAT 0.1G)
PROTEIN 0.1G   CARBOHYDRATE 4.2G
CHOLESTEROL 0MG   SODIUM 0MG

MOCHA FUDGE SAUCE

1 tablespoon margarine
1 (1-ounce) square unsweetened chocolate
¼ cup sugar
3 tablespoons unsweetened cocoa
2 teaspoons instant coffee granules
1 teaspoon cornstarch
½ cup dark corn syrup
¼ cup skim milk
1 tablespoon Kahlúa or other coffee-flavored liqueur (optional)
1 teaspoon vanilla extract

Combine margarine and chocolate in a small saucepan; cook over low heat until chocolate melts, stirring occasionally. Combine sugar and next 3 ingredients in a small bowl. Add corn syrup and milk, stirring with a wire whisk until blended; add to saucepan. Bring to a boil over medium heat, and cook 1 minute, stirring constantly. Remove from heat, and stir in Kahlúa, if desired, and vanilla.

Serve sauce warm, or cover surface of mixture with plastic wrap and chill. Serve over nonfat ice cream or frozen yogurt. Yield: 1 cup.

PER TABLESPOON: 67 CALORIES (24% FROM FAT)
FAT 1.8G (SATURATED FAT 0.8G)
PROTEIN 0.7G   CARBOHYDRATE 12.7G
CHOLESTEROL 0MG   SODIUM 23MG

FYI

What if you don't have Kahlúa or some other liqueur called for in the recipe? Don't worry—your results will usually be just fine if you substitute an equal amount of another liquid (fruit juice or water) along with an appropriate extract for flavor. For more information on alcohol substitutions, see the chart on page 10.

Mocha Fudge Sauce and Vanilla Ice Milk (page 90)

Chocolate-Cherry Sauce

CHOCOLATE-CHERRY SAUCE

2 tablespoons sugar
1 tablespoon cornstarch
2 tablespoons unsweetened cocoa
1 cup skim milk
2 tablespoons light-colored corn syrup
1 tablespoon cherry brandy (optional)
½ teaspoon vanilla extract
2 tablespoons chopped dried cherries

Combine first 3 ingredients in a saucepan. Gradually stir in milk, corn syrup, and brandy, if desired. Cook over medium heat, stirring constantly, 8 minutes or until thickened. Remove from heat; stir in vanilla and cherries. Serve warm or at room temperature over nonfat ice cream. Yield: 1⅓ cups.

PER TABLESPOON: 24 CALORIES (8% FROM FAT)
FAT 0.2G (SATURATED FAT 0.1G)
PROTEIN 0.6G   CARBOHYDRATE 5.0G
CHOLESTEROL 0MG   SODIUM 8MG

MISSISSIPPI MUD SAUCE

⅓ cup miniature marshmallows
1 tablespoon cornstarch
2 tablespoons unsweetened cocoa
1 cup skim milk
1 tablespoon light-colored corn syrup
1 teaspoon vanilla extract
¼ teaspoon ground cinnamon
¼ cup miniature marshmallows
1 tablespoon chopped pecans

Combine first 3 ingredients in a small saucepan. Gradually stir in milk and corn syrup. Cook over medium heat, stirring constantly, until thickened. Remove from heat; stir in vanilla and cinnamon. Let cool. Stir in ¼ cup marshmallows and pecans. Serve over nonfat ice cream, angel food cake, or fresh fruit. Yield: 1 cup.

PER TABLESPOON: 23 CALORIES (16% FROM FAT)
FAT 0.4G (SATURATED FAT 0.1G)
PROTEIN 0.8G   CARBOHYDRATE 3.9G
CHOLESTEROL 0MG   SODIUM 11MG

INDEX